9075

745.5 Raymo, Anne

Sew Up Art

DATE DUE			
JA 19 '84			
AUG 1 '91			

By Anne Raymo

100 Ways to Have Fun With an Alligator & 100 Other Involving Art Projects
(in collaboration with Norman Laliberté, Richey Kehl, and Alex Mogelon)

Sew-Up Art

How To Do It

26 Appliqué Projects

by
Anne Raymo
and
Holly Vose

Photographs
by
Jim Raymo

quick fox

New York
London

Imperial Public Library
Imperial, Texas

Copyright © Anne Raymo and Holly Vose, 1976
All rights reserved.

International Standard Book Number: 0-8256-3065-7
Library of Congress Catalog Card Number: 75-45768
Printed in the United States of America.

No part of this book may be reproduced or transmitted in any form
or by any means, electronic or mechanical, including photocopying,
without permission in writing from the publisher: Quick Fox, A Division
of Music Sales Corporation, 33 West 60 Street, New York 10023.

In Great Britain: Book Sales Ltd., 78 Newman Street, London W1, England.
In Canada: Gage Trade Publishing, P. O. Box 5000, 164 Commander Blvd.,
Agincourt, Ontario M1S 3C7.

Book and cover design by Antupit & Others.

Contents

6	Introduction	34	Projects
8	Tools	36	Patches
10	Glossary	38	Jacket
12	How To Do It	40	Belt
	Fabrics to use	42	Necklace
	Backing	44	Tie
	Thread	46	Vest
	Stuffing	48	Dress
	Pressing	50	Handbag
	Cutting the fabric	52	Tennis-Racket Cover
	Pinning the design	54	Mask
	Sewing the design in place	56	Costume
	Quilting	58	Pillow
	Finishing the edges	60	Quilt
	Stitches	64	Headboard
20	How To See It	66	Standing Screen
22	Calling Up the Image	68	Doll
24	Drawing by Ear	72	Flag
26	Shedding Light on the Subject	74	Child's Project
28	Seeing	76	Valentine
30	Capturing the Eye	78	Poem Piece
32	Patterns you can trace and re-use	80	Games
	Section of color photographs	82	Photo Collage
		84	Family Portrait
		86	Personal Memento
		88	Diary/Book Cover
		90	Wall Hanging
		94	Credits

Introduction

The language we will use in this book is craft. It is one that allows us to communicate on nonverbal levels, and what is communicated is always new.

Craft is a language that speaks through the attention we give to the things we do. It speaks through the way we adorn ourselves and our dwellings. It speaks through the way we care for the "handmade" vibration in the things we give ourselves and others. It speaks to the heart.

The craft we are talking about here is appliqué, the process of applying one fabric shape to another. We will describe the various ways to do it and show you the projects we have done. We hope you will try ours and create your own.

LET YOUR IMAGINATION PLAY FREELY

and you will find that images and ideas flow. The great pleasure of working in this medium is the unlimited freedom one has in choosing colors, patterns, and textures from the wide, ever-changing selection of available materials.

APPLIQUÉ

is an easy technique to learn, and to develop the skills takes little time. It's a wonderful way to brighten yourself and your surroundings, and

it's fun to do!

The craft has been simplified greatly by the development of the zigzag sewing machine. The fine and exact stitchery that can make appliqué time-consuming may be done quickly and with precision on the machine. The sewing machine makes things faster! This is not to discourage those who wish to work by hand. Taking the time and attention necessary to apply your designs by hand will greatly enhance the beauty of the final result. The richness of a hand-embroidered piece is difficult to match on the machine. The projects and exercises in this book may be done either on the machine or by hand.

However you decide to work, regard your hands, the machine, the scissors, the cloth as your accomplices. Be aware that the materials have a life of their own; the varicolored threads and cloth are natural stimulants to the eye and the imagination. Enjoy the learning process involved in this unfolding relationship between fabric and cutter, craft and maker. The language reveals itself.

One lives within
the spirit of
transformation and
not in the act.

Henry Miller

Tools

Zigzag sewing machine (optional, but helpful)
Fabrics
Threads
Scissors
Pins and needles
Stuffing
Glue
Assorted decorative items: beads, bells, ribbon, studs, charms, etc.

Appliqué is a wonderful exercise in imagination. You can copy a design if you like, or use someone else's design to take off from; the nicest, however, is to dream up your own. One way to go about doing this is to lay out the article of clothing, or whatever is to be appliquéd, and look at it carefully. Try to see the design that particular shape or object calls for.

If you're patient, you'll find that you can develop the knack of doing this. Everyone can make beautiful, unique things; it's a question of taking the

When you begin a project, take the time to give it your full attention. Put everything else out of your mind and enjoy the colors and textures you are working with. We find it nice to work each time in the same

Create a pleasant place to work. Find a room or a corner where you can spread the fabrics out all around you. It's good to work on a low table or on the floor, so that you can view the project as a whole as you work on it. Allow the materials to inspire you; they will play a major part in the designing.

thread: a filament ... a slender stream ... a streak of light or color ... something continuous or drawn out ... a train of thought ... to pass into or through something ... to make one's way ...

Webster's New Collegiate Dictionary

Glossary

Appliqué: "to put on: a cutout decoration fastened to a larger piece of material: to apply to a larger surface: OVERLAY" (Webster's New Collegiate Dictionary)

Backing: a piece of fabric placed behind the fabric that is being appliquéd, to give it more body and to make the machine zigzag stitch run smoother

Baste: to sew with long loose stitches in order to hold something in place temporarily

Bias: the diagonal of the fabric, i.e. a line at a 45° angle to the selvage

Clip: to make tiny cuts on the concave or inside curved edge of a fabric shape; used to "ease" a curved edge. Clips should be made up to but not through the stitching line (see illustration on page 16)

Embroider: to decorate any fabric with needlework, either by hand or by machine

Grommets: metal rings used to reinforce holes made for hanging a fabric

Knotting: sewing together two or more layers of material by means of single stitches drawn through and back and tied; most commonly used in quilting, to attach the front to the lining and hold the inner padding in place (see illustration on page 62)

Mitering: one way to turn a corner neatly when binding a finished piece. At the corners, a diagonal seam runs from the inside angle to the outside corner of the binding material (see page 63 for illustration)

Notch: to make tiny triangular-shaped cuts on the convex or outside curved edge of a fabric shape; notches should be made up to but not through the stitching line (see illustration on page 16)

Quilting: two layers of fabric with padding in between, held together by stitched designs done either by hand or by machine

Shrinking: the loss of the original shape and size of any applied fabric because of the gathering tendency of the satin stitch

Straight and grain: the warp and weft threads of a woven fabric (warp threads run the length of the fabric and the weft threads run across, from selvage to selvage)

Tension: the tightness of the top thread and the bobbin thread on a sewing machine

Trapunto: high relief made by inserting stuffing between two layers of fabric (see illustration on page 64)

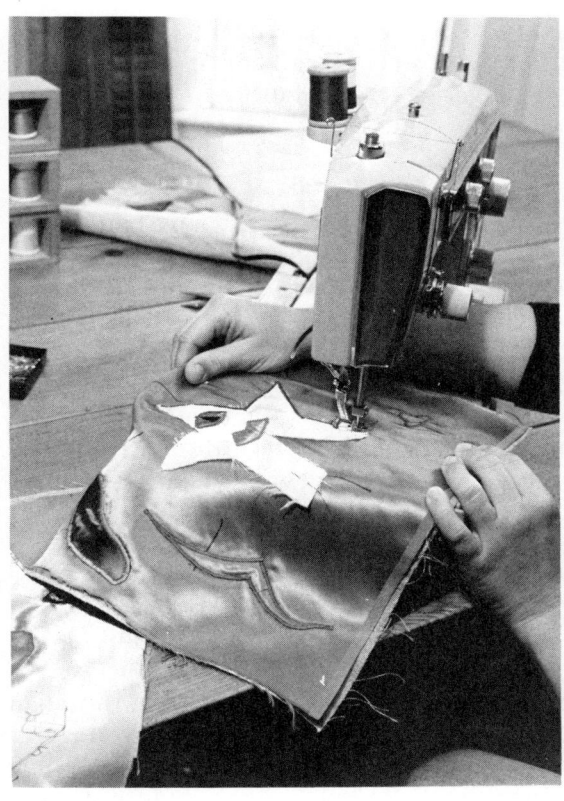 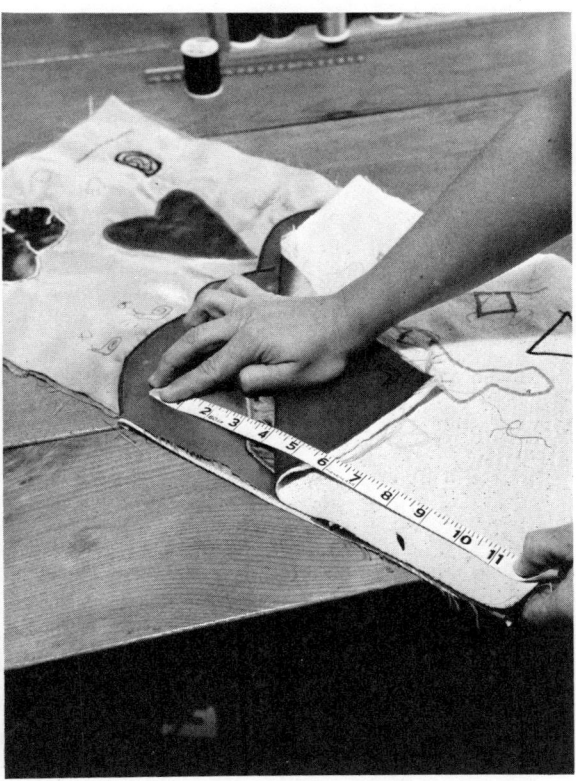

Craft: skill in planning, making or executing: DEXTERITY ... skill in deceiving to gain an end ... a boat ... AIRCRAFT ... SPACECRAFT syn see ART ... to make by or as if by hand

Webster's New Collegiate Dictionary

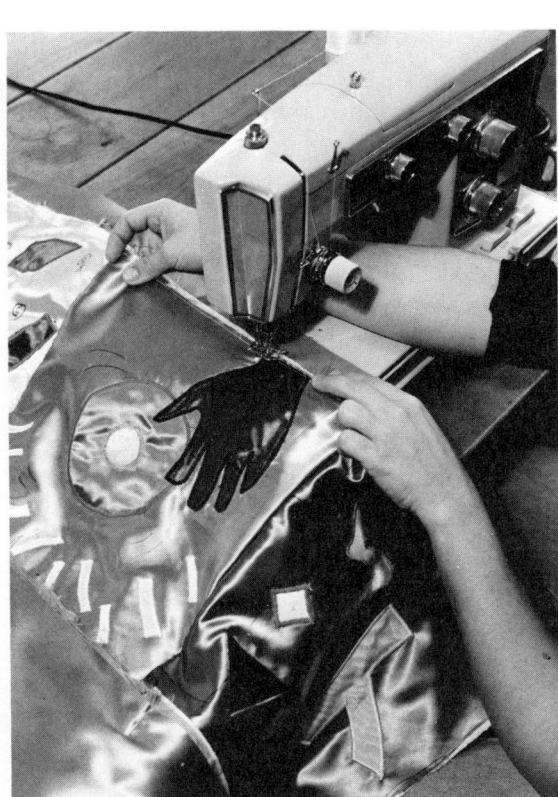 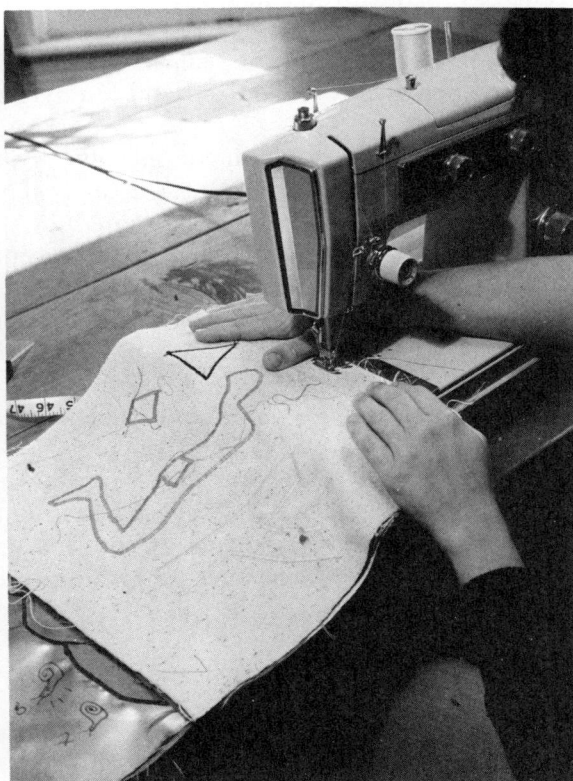

How To Do It

Fabrics to use: When choosing fabrics for appliqué, don't hesitate to mix and experiment with different prints and colors and a variety of weights and textures. Let things happen on their own. Combining bright solid colors and ornate prints or layering several fabrics of different textures will add richness to any design.

The fabrics you choose to apply as cutouts can be almost anything—solid colors or prints; cottons, satins, woolens, velvets, flannels, or felts. Knits, loose weaves, silks, any fabrics that are very thin or very heavy should be avoided; they are difficult to cut and sew. For things you plan to wash, be sure that all of your applied fabrics are colorfast, washable, and preshrunk. On things that may need only an occasional dry cleaning, you can use the fancier fabrics.

When appliquéing clothes, it is important to apply durable fabrics at points of special wear, like the seat of a pair of pants or the elbows of a jacket. Heavy cottons and denims serve well, but for unusual prints in this weight try rummaging through upholstery shops. They may have remnants of colorful prints, or perhaps old swatch cards with samples of out-of-date styles that you could use for smaller patches and designs.

It's especially nice to work with old or used fabrics that have history in them, but be sure they are not too worn. There are innumerable places to explore for fabrics other than your local sewing center, department store, or variety store. Poke around in antique or junk shops, at yard sales or rummage sales, and you'll undoubtedly find an old dress, or slipcover, or faded drapery. Often Goodwill or Salvation Army centers will have 1940s dresses, Hawaiian shirts, upholstery fabric, and the like. These places are sources for materials that you won't find in fabric shops, and you can usually buy them for practically nothing. Even if something is torn or faded, you'll still be able to salvage enough to use for patches or details of decoration. Save scraps; you can always find a use for them!

The general rule in choosing fabrics is to use the colors and textures that are the most attractive and personal to you. My friend Jan dyes and tie-dyes the fabrics she works with.

Backing: All appliqué work done on the machine with light- and medium-weight materials (cottons, satins, some wools, velvets, etc.) is easier if you use a backing material under the cloth you are sewing the cutouts onto. *This does not apply to hand-sewn appliqué.* The backing keeps the zigzag stitching smooth and helps prevent "shrinking" (pieces losing their original shape and size because of the pull of the stitching). The most effective backing materials are tightly woven and a good medium weight, for example canvas, linen, heavy cotton, and unbleached muslin. I use inexpensive canvas or cotton duck purchased at a discount art supply store.

On denims, felt, heavy wools and linens—any rather heavy materials—backing is unnecessary.

Thread: There is a variety of threads one can use. Any cotton or polyester thread will serve most of your needs. Silk thread is wonderful to use, its sheen is very elegant; however, it's expensive and sometimes difficult to find. If you find yourself wholeheartedly into appliqué and doing a lot of sewing, you can look for local thread wholesalers who will sell you large spindles of thread at great savings.

When sewing by hand you can use embroidery threads for extra richness.

Stuffing: If you decide to experiment with the third dimension, cotton batting, polyester fill, and shredded foam are good for stuffing behind the applied fabric shape. Scraps and old nylon stockings may also be used. This is called trapunto.

Scissors can acquire more feeling for line than pencils or charcoal.

Henri Matisse

Polyester fill seems to be the best thing to use for quilting; it is washable and doesn't bunch up the way cotton battings tend to. An old blanket may also be used (check first for washability).

To stuff dolls, or other small objects, use whatever is available: for example, cotton batting, polyester fill, shredded foam, scraps, or old stockings.

Pressing: Keep an iron close by as you work. Press each piece before you cut it if necessary. It's easiest to work with cloth that is flat and neat. Press on the wrong side of the fabric or use a press cloth between the iron and the fabric when working with delicate materials.

Cutting the fabric: It's most important to use scissors that are easy to handle and make sharp clean cuts. Nothing is more frustrating than trying to work with dull scissors.

The beginner should try to stick to large bold shapes. Richness and detail can be achieved by the use of many textures, colors, and prints. I like to cut the shape directly from the fabric. This takes some practice, but as you master it you'll find it allows you to think with the scissors, and the unexpected often happens. If you find you prefer sketching or tracing your designs first onto the fabric, by all means do so.

Cutting for hand sewing: See page 16 for details.

Cutting strips: For long, straight strips of fabric, it is best to cut along the straight or grain of the textile, not across it. This will make the edges of the cutout easier to work with and less likely to ravel or pull out of the satin stitch.

Cutting curved shapes: Cutting along the bias of the fabric will make the shape easy to bend and twist to your needs.

Making two sides at once: It is possible to appliqué two sides of a piece at the same time. Instructions for this are given for the Flag; however, it is somewhat complicated and not recommended to the beginner.

Pinning the design: After the images are cut out, place them on the background and arrange and rearrange them until they take the shape you are looking for. When you are pleased with the design and feel it's complete, you are ready to pin.

Whenever possible, pin together small sections, sew these separately, and then attach to the background.

For machine sewing, pin the shape well within the sewing line, so that the pins will not get in the way of the needle. When it is necessary to pin along the edge, place the pins at right angles to the sewing line, so that the needle can easily sew over them.

Small pieces used for details can be glued to their backings.

Sewing the design in place: **By machine:** After the design has been conceived, cut out, and pinned or glued in place, the piece is ready for the machine. Understand your sewing machine. We find machines vary in their performance. The beginner should approach the machine with patience and realize it takes some time to get the feel of it.

Material: the elements, constituents, or substances of which something is composed or can be made ... matter that has qualities which give it individuality and by which it may be categorized ... data that may be worked into a more finished form ...

Webster's New Collegiate Dictionary

Be aware of stitch width and tension, and choose the settings that are best for your project. Use narrow zigzag settings for detailing, wide settings for bold images. On most machines you can vary the width of the stitch to suit your needs as you sew. Be sure to use stitches that are wide enough to securely sew the image to the backing. Adjust the tension of the stitch to accommodate the thickness of the fabric and the type of stitch you are using.

With the machine foot down, the fabric should move easily under the needle, but on heavier fabrics, it sometimes helps to gently pull the fabric from behind the foot. You will maintain best stitch control when you sew at a moderate and consistent speed.

To sew curves, circles, or any large strips or shapes, baste the piece in place before satin stitching. This is important to remember, as the zigzag stitch tends to "shrink" the cloth and a finished piece may end up shorter than your original measure. Basting beforehand will minimize this.

To stitch a corner or any sharp turn, sew up to the turning point; then, with the needle down through the fabric, lift the pressure foot and pivot the fabric to the new direction. Lower the foot and continue sewing.

By hand: If you wish to sew your appliqué by hand, there are a few basic stitches you'll want to know: the running stitch, the hemstitch, and one or two embroidery stitches (e.g. the buttonhole stitch, the herringbone stitch) should cover all your needs. These and several other decorative stitches are illustrated on page 19; using them will add a marvelous quality to your finished appliqué.

There are two ways to go about hand appliqué:
1. All designs to be applied can be cut with a 3/16" (approximately) hem allowance all round. The hem is clipped, tucked under, and pinned in place. (Some people like to baste the hem and iron the pieces before sewing in place.) The shape is then tacked to the background with a straight stitch or hemstitch. An embroidery stitch may be used to decorate the finished appliqué.

cut out here   notch and clip, turn under, stitch

2. You can eliminate the steps of adding and turning under hem allowance by cutting the designs exactly the size you want them and then running a touch of white glue (the kind that dries clear) thinly and evenly along the raw edges to keep them from raveling. Attach

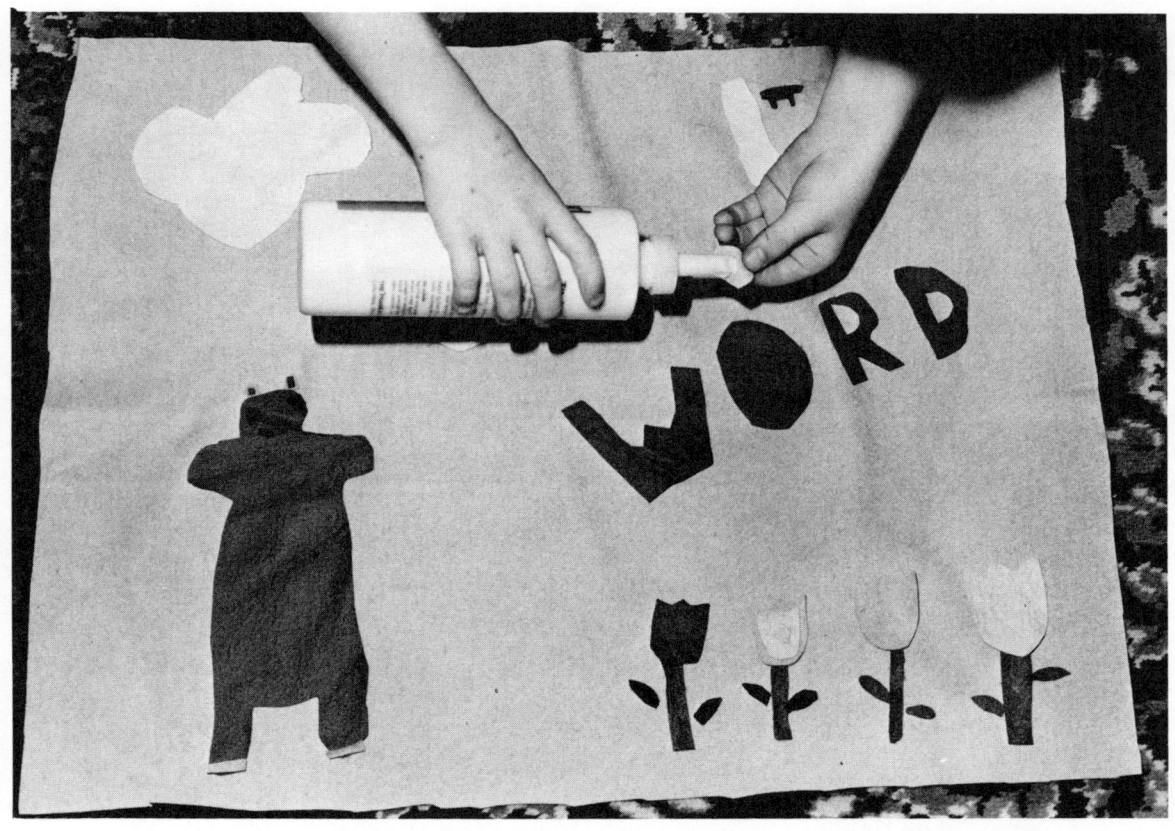

Pin: a piece of solid material used esp. for fastening separate articles together . . . the center peg of a target; also: the center itself . . . a peg for regulating the tension of the strings of a musical instrument . . . the part of a key stem that enters a lock . . . to hold fast . . .

Webster's New Collegiate Dictionary

the shapes to whatever you are making with a buttonhole stitch (or herringbone, featherstitch, or other), as illustrated. This, of course, is not practical for items that will be washed.

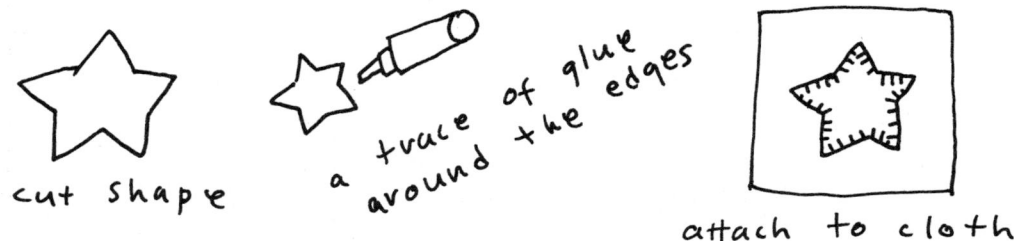

Quilting: This is the process of joining a top piece and a lining together with a layer of padding in between, by means of stitching designs. Use a polyester filling (or flannel, or an old blanket). Pin and then baste the layers you are quilting together (this is fully described in the Quilt), then trace your quilting designs onto the cloth with tailor's chalk.

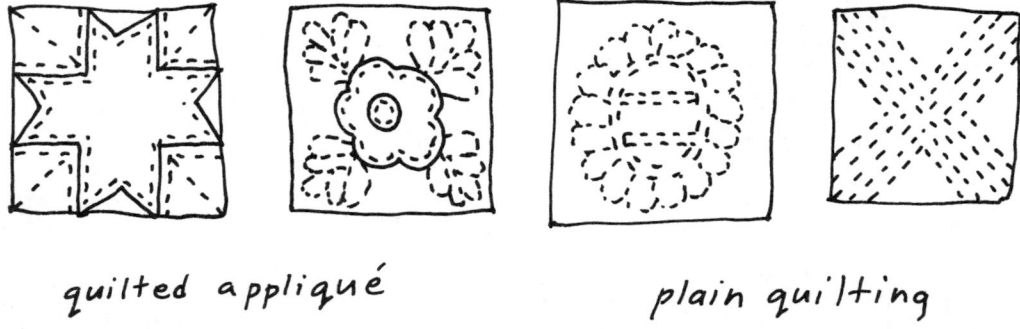

Sew along these lines, catching all three layers with a neat running stitch. Small pieces may be quilted by machine with a straight stitch. Some sewing machines have quilting attachments.

Finishing the edges: The edges of a finished piece may be simply turned under and hemstitched; or for more elaborate linings and finishes see Quilt and Wall Hanging.

An excellent and inexpensive book that I recommend to the novice for more expanded explanations of sewing techniques is *Quilting and Patchwork* (Sunset Books).

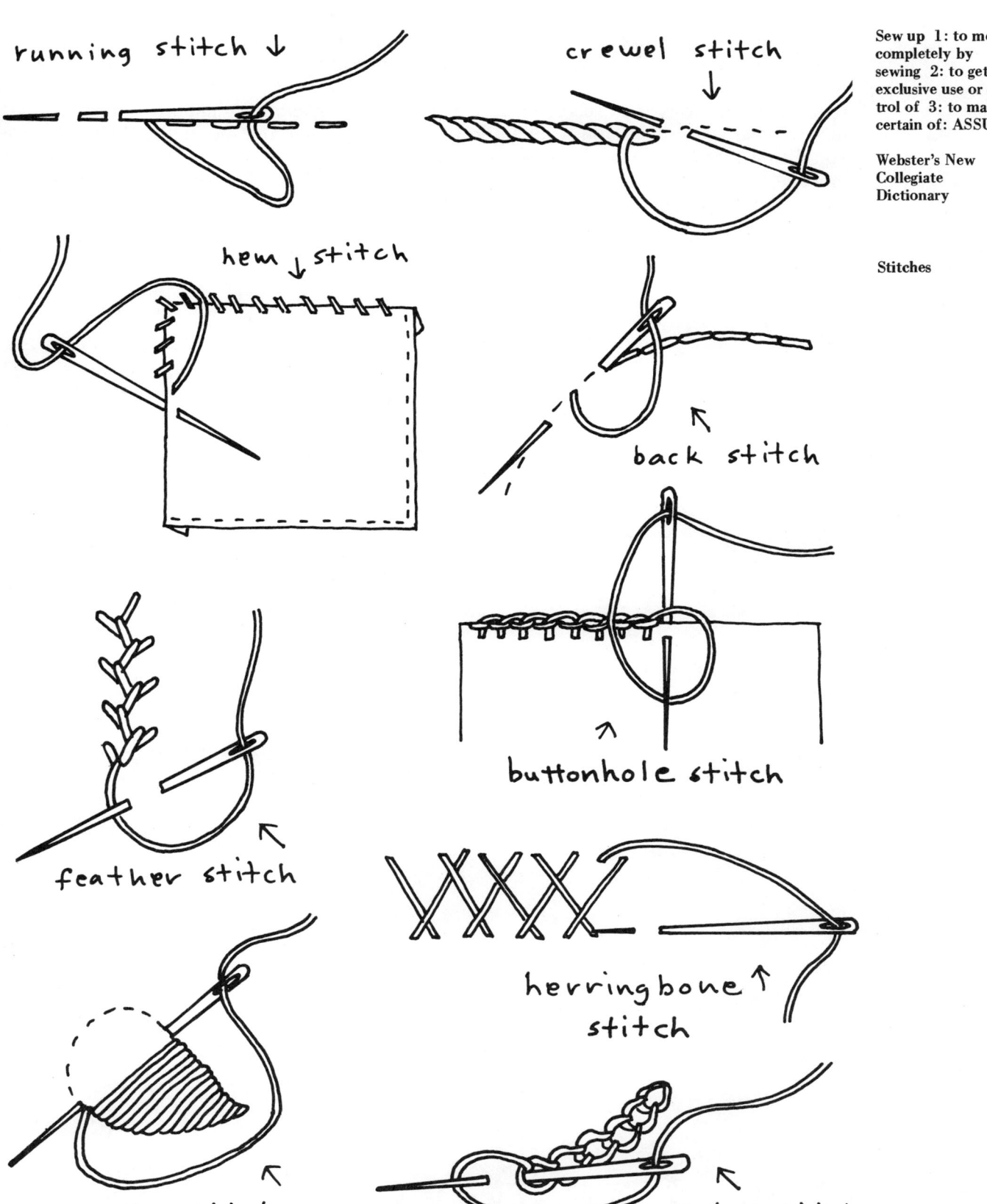

Sew up 1: to mend completely by sewing 2: to get exclusive use or control of 3: to make certain of: ASSURE

Webster's New Collegiate Dictionary

Stitches

How To See It

In my conversations with others I find that the reason most people hesitate to take up some visual form of self-expression is a lack of confidence in their ability to dream up images to work with. Many find it boring to copy designs and yet don't know how to go about finding their own. The trick is to relax; let ideas come to you. Everyone's mind is a storehouse of images. Bear the project you want to do in mind, then wait and see—with a little patience you'll find that designs occur to you. What follows is a series of exercises that may help you practice this, to be done with others or by yourself. The object of the exercises is simply enjoyment; to realize the essential playfulness of the creative act.

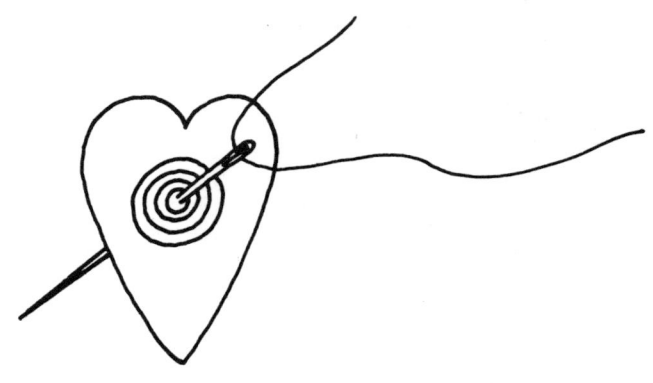

Many have original minds who do not think it—they are led away by Custom—Now it appears to me that almost any man may like the Spider spin from his own inwards his own airy Citadel—the points of leaves and twigs on which the Spider begins her work are few, and she fills the Air with a beautiful circuiting . . .

John Keats

Calling Up the Image

Suggested materials: pencil and paper; fabrics (solid-color cottons or satins); scissors; thread; pins. Or: construction or other colored papers; glue.

Relax. Clear your mind.

Rest like this for a few moments, then write down the first image that occurs to you.

Now clear your head.

After a few moments, again write down the first image that occurs to you. Do this five times.

If two people are working together, each choose five images.

For example:

Jo (age 8)	Anne
"Lightning Lad"	"Dog"
"Saturn Girl"	"Ark"
"Someone getting married"	"Water"
"Someone swimming"	"Mind"
"A monster"	"Heart"

Make a picture, cutting these images out of cloth or paper and arranging them on a background. If an image comes as a scene, e.g. "people getting married," you can use a symbol (ring).

Glue, or pin and sew (see Wall Hanging for sewing details).

Art like love is an active process of growth and development, not a God-given talent...

Robert Motherwell

Drawing by Ear

Suggested materials: fabrics (solid-color cottons or satins); scissors; thread, pins. Or: scissors; construction paper, origami paper, or other colored paper; glue. Try this in black and white too.

Spread out the materials and sit quietly. Open your senses. Be utterly silent.

Choose a sound. Let it be the first sound that occurs to you.

Make the sound. Notice where it vibrates in your body. Notice how the vibration moves and changes as you raise and lower the tone.

Repeat this sound quietly to yourself for a minute or two, then begin your picture. Have no preconceived thought of what the picture should look like. While you dream up the images, repeat the chosen sound to yourself.

Let your picture reflect the sound.

Glue, or pin and sew the pieces in place (see Wall Hanging for sewing details).

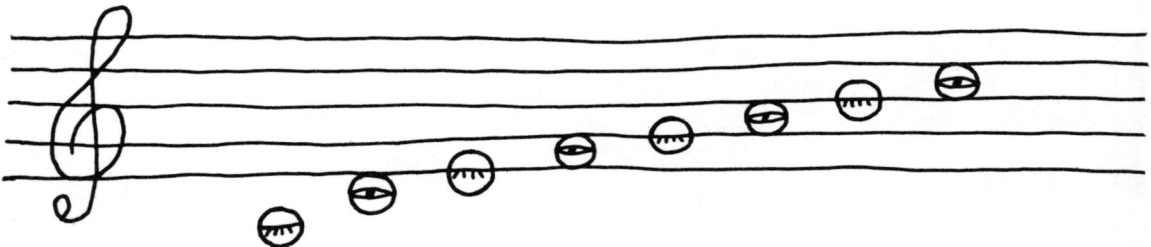

Variation: As many people as you wish can work together. Each takes the sound of a note on the scale. Each person reflects this sound in images, working in the way described above.

The indians long ago knew that music was going on permanently and that hearing it was like looking out a window at a landscape which didn't stop when one turned away.

John Cage

Shedding Light on the Subject

Begin. Hang a picture (or object) that pleases you in a place where you can view it clearly, easily.

Look at the picture. Think of yourself as being the source of light in which the picture is viewed.

rest

Think of the object as being the source of the light in which it is viewed.

rest

Think of your eyes as reflecting the image you see.

rest

Think of your eyes as absorbing the image you see.

rest

Imagine you see with your hands.

Imagine you see with your whole body.

See the whole picture at once. Practice looking at the picture all at once, keeping your focus on the whole.

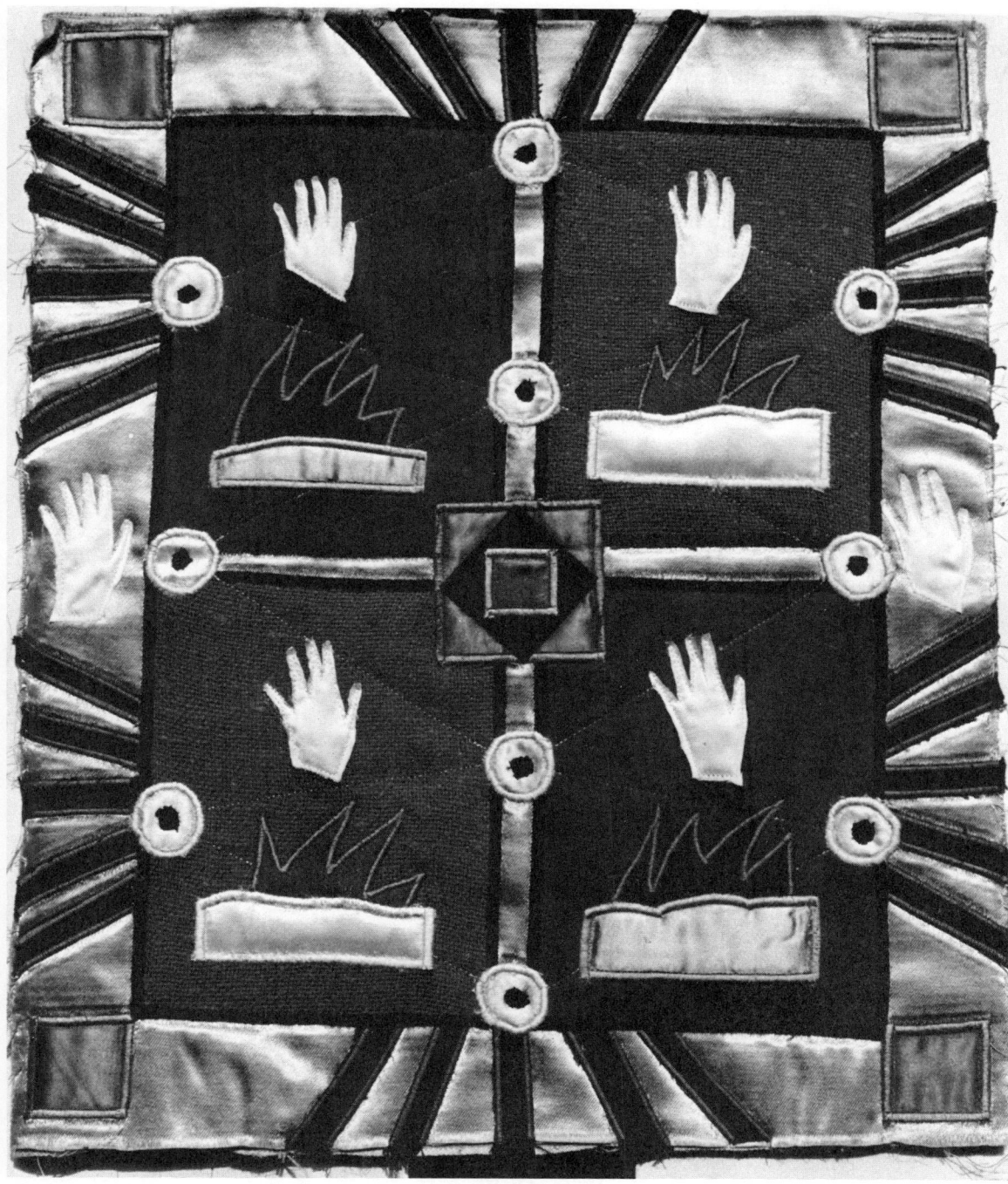

To see is to forget the name of the thing one sees.

Paul Valéry

Seeing

Suggested materials: fabrics (solid-color cottons are good to work with). Or: construction or other colored paper and glue. This is a nice exercise to do in black and white, as well as color. Do it with someone by alternating images.

Cut out a series of nine squares or rectangles the same size.

Create a picture in each shape by putting an image that appeals to you in #1, then put the image the first image brings to mind in #2, and so on to #9. Return to #1 and begin again with another image.

After you have two or three images in each square, arrange all the squares and add any details you feel would help tie them all together into a nice picture. Glue or sew all the pieces together. If you are sewing, see Quilt for sewing details.

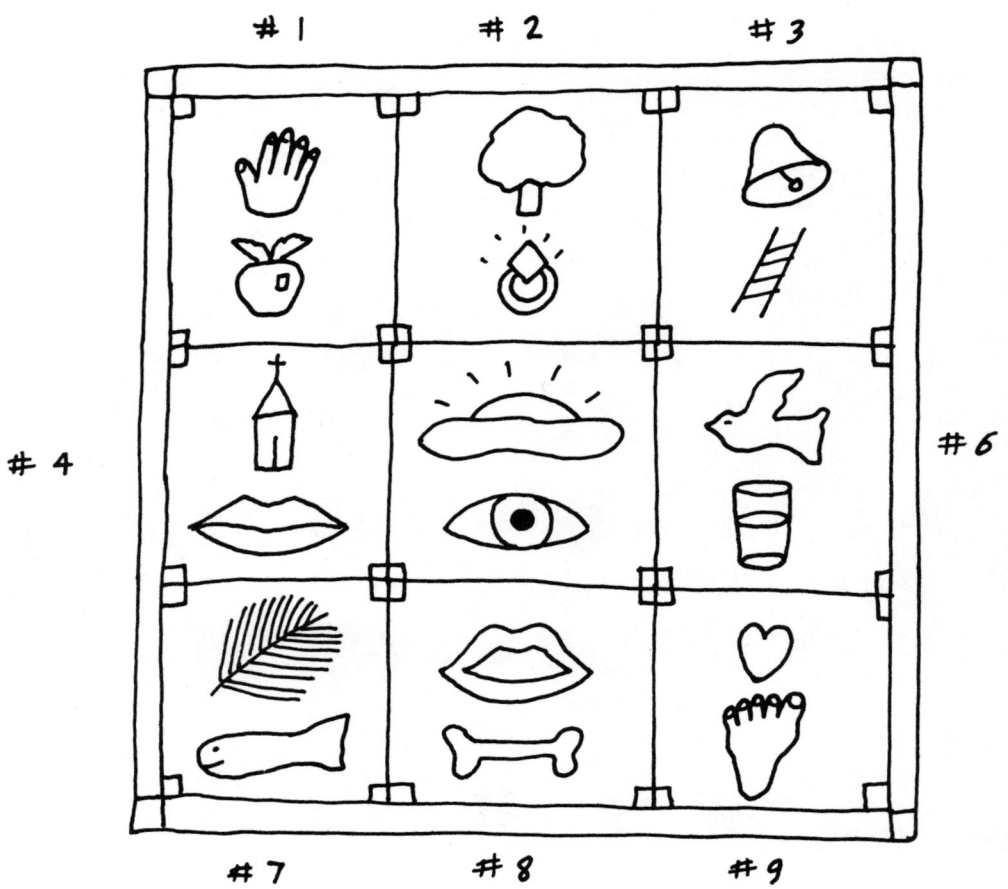

The critical moment is my act of seeing. The rest is the patient reconstruction of this hallucination and successive hallucinations which arise in the course of making. The contribution of subject matter is almost a side effect since what I see is not the thing itself but—myself—in its form.

Claes Oldenburg

Capturing the Eye

Suggested materials: Fabrics (solid-color cottons or satins—have a choice of as many colors as possible). Or: colored papers; glue.

Spread the materials out before you. Cut a large piece for the background. After resting your eyes for a few minutes, choose the color that appeals to you the most, at that moment. Now, cut quickly from the cloth the shape of the first image that color evokes in your imagination.

Lay that shape on the background and rest your eyes for a moment.

Choose the next color that attracts you. Again, cut out the shape of the image that color suggests to you, and add it to the background. Continue in this way until you have six shapes.

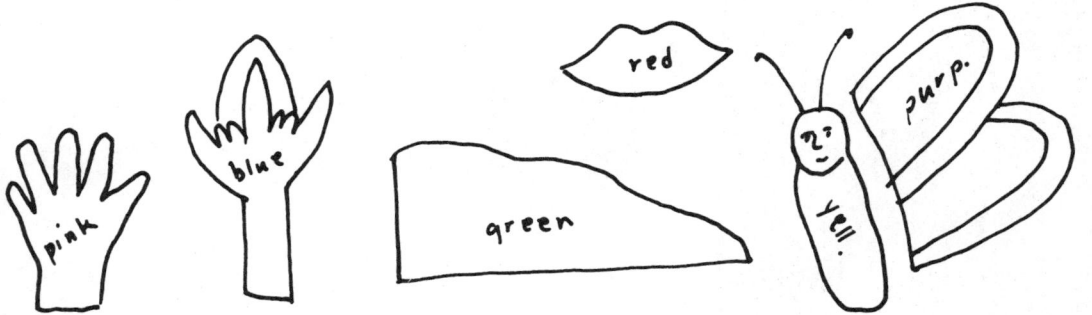

Now, look carefully at those images. Let them suggest a story or subject to you. Complete the picture by adding the details that tell your story. Glue, or pin and sew the design in place.

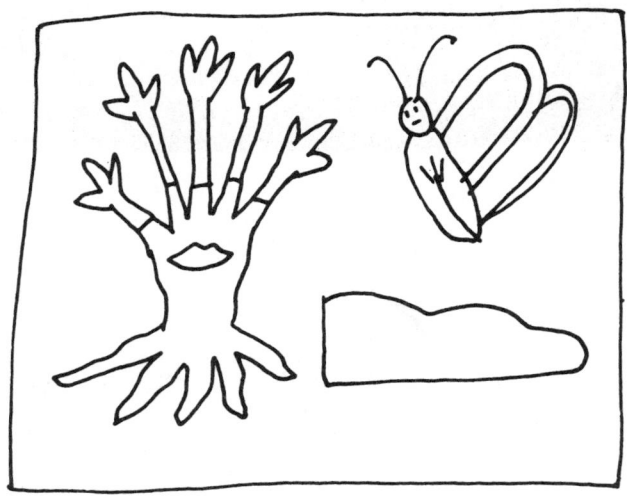

A book to help you with visualization: *Seeing with the Mind's Eye: The History, Techniques and Uses of Visualization* by Mike Samuels, M.D., and Nancy Samuels (Bookworks/Random House).

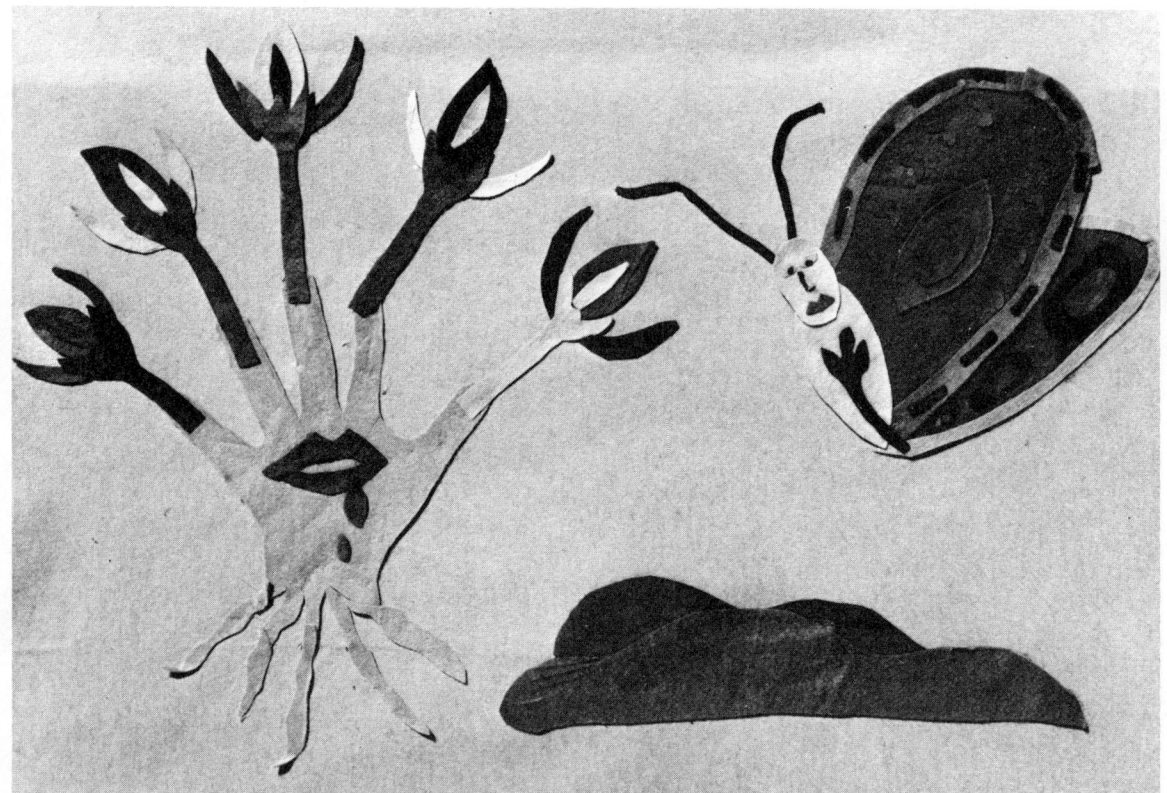

And now an altogether revolutionary discovery: to adapt one-self to the contents of the paintbox is more important than nature and its study. I must some day be able to improvise freely on the chromatic keyboard of the watercolor cups.

Paul Klee

It's fun to make patterns of your favorite shapes and use them over as repeating elements in your designs. Here are some of the ones I use; make up your own as well. To use a pattern, first trace the shape onto a sheet of paper; cut out that shape, and then trace around the cutout onto your chosen fabric.

Karen made this baby quilt with assorted calicos to celebrate the birth of her daughter, p. 60.

Headboard made with felt and trapunto stuffing, p. 64.

Both quilts combine appliqué centers with patchwork, p. 60.

Cotton pillow with appliqué and free-floating ribbons, 15″ x 15″, p. 58.

Patchwork pillow; pillow with trapunto-stuffed ribs, p. 58.

Holly's jacket of satin appliqué, p. 38.

Cotton mask with satin appliqué and gold metallic threads, p. 54.

Billy's jacket with circle patch, assorted ribbons, and horse pattern, p. 38.

Anne's jacket of satin and cotton appliqué, p. 38.

Jacket decorated with shells, studs, charms, ribbons, medals, and appliqué of flowers cut from a bold chintz material, p. 38.

Patches of assorted cottons and satins, p. 36.

Natasha's satin wall hanging, p. 90.

Child's project made of felt and glue, pp. 30, 74.

Ties of satin appliqué, p. 44.

Family portrait: photo screen on satin with appliqué and embroidery, p. 84.

Christmas wall hanging made of felt and glue, with plastic and sequined decorations, p. 90.

Standing screen made with felt appliqué, p. 66.

Satin valentine with sequined hearts, pp. 76, 88.

Dress of satin appliqué, p. 48.

Poem piece, in cottons, illustrating lines from W. B. Yeats, p. 78.

7' x 3' wall hanging made with wools, velvets, and cottons, p. 90.

Reversible flag made with weather-resistant fabrics, p. 72.

Necklace of stuffed satin shapes attached to silk cord, p. 42.

33

Projects

All general instructions are given for machine sewing. If you are working by hand, see page 16 for help with adapting details.

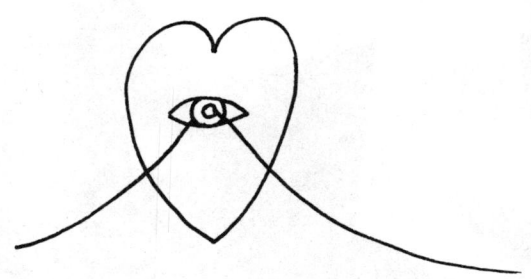

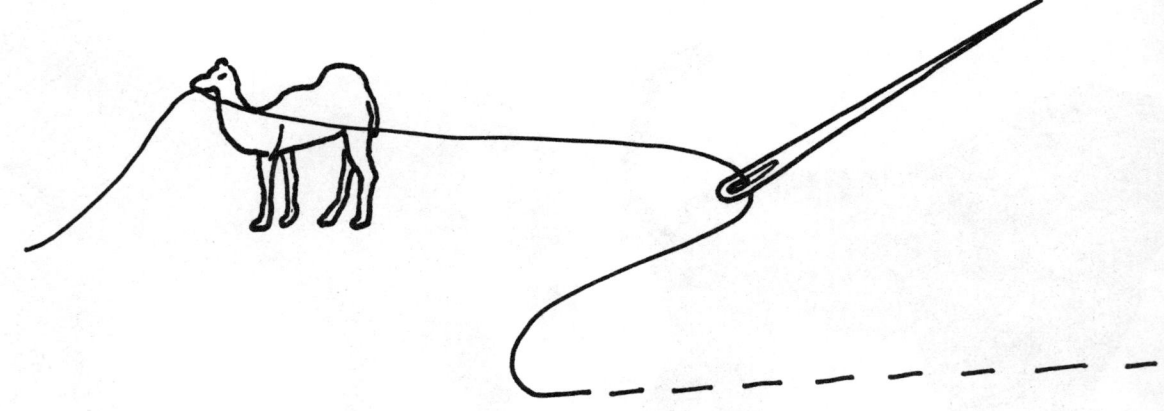

While I work I leave my body outside the door, the way Moslems take off their shoes before entering the mosque.

Picasso

Patches

You need: Fabric scraps (for patches that you will put on washable things, use washable fabric; if you plan to apply the patch to something that may need only an occasional dry cleaning, try a combination of cottons and vibrant satins and velvets); a small amount of backing material.

Proceed:

1 Cut a piece of backing fabric (canvas or heavy cotton), slightly larger than the patch size you want.

2 Cut the elements of your patch design and place them on the backing. You can either let part of the backing show as background, or cover it completely.

You may want to use the patterns in this book (see pages 32 and 33); or, use this simple project as a chance to practice your own design skills. For the best effects, always work with shapes or symbols that are particularly pleasing to you. It's good to keep the outside edges of your shape simple; this makes it easy to sew the patch onto whatever you are decorating.

3 When you are happy with the arrangement, pin all the pieces in place and sew with a satin stitch.

4 Cut away the excess backing fabric along the outside stitch line as closely as possible, taking care not to cut into the stitching.

5 Now pin the patch onto whatever you like and sew over the edges with a wide close satin stitch. If you are using the patch to cover a hole in your clothing, mend the hole first, then apply the patch.

There are any number of ways to use your patches. Apply them to jeans, jackets, curtains, director's chairs, a handbag, a hat, or a pillow. Make them for your friends and exchange them. Perhaps make a jacket with a patch on it from each of your friends—a variation on the old friendship quilt idea.

I would suggest (as an exercise) that sometime you take your two eyes along with you—and leave your intellect—and your friends' intellects at home —you might— without these handicaps begin to see things—that would surprise you.

John Marin

Jacket

You need: A denim jacket, or something of similar weight (perhaps a heavy workshirt or a khaki jacket) —if the jacket is new, wash it a number of times to soften it before you begin; fabric scraps; Army surplus patches, ribbons, buttons, medals, studs, sequins are good added decoration.

Proceed:

1 Study the jacket carefully, front and back, and try to see a design that enhances its lines. You may find it helpful to make a sketch of your ideas.

A simple approach is to make a series of patches which can then be sewn onto the jacket. (It is easier to work on a small area when you can, rather than maneuvering the entire jacket through the machine.) You might try making a large circular patch for the back of the jacket.

2 Complete the laying out of your design and pin all the elements in place.

3 Sew all the pieces on the front and back, using a satin stitch. Attach any designs to the sleeves by hand; or you can, if you wish, open the seams of the sleeves, sew on the appliqué by machine, then reclose the seams. (Some new machines have a special narrow sewing surface for sleeves.) It's nice to edge the collar and the cuffs with velvet or satin ribbons, attached with a featherstitch; or add studs, ready-made patches, etc., as you please.

4 You can embroider your name, or any words that may have special meaning for you, on your jacket in bright-colored cotton or metallic threads. If you are working with a sewing machine, place the stitch setting at "embroider" and proceed according to the instructions provided with your particular machine. It's best to practice "writing" several times on scrap cloth before attempting it on the finished piece.

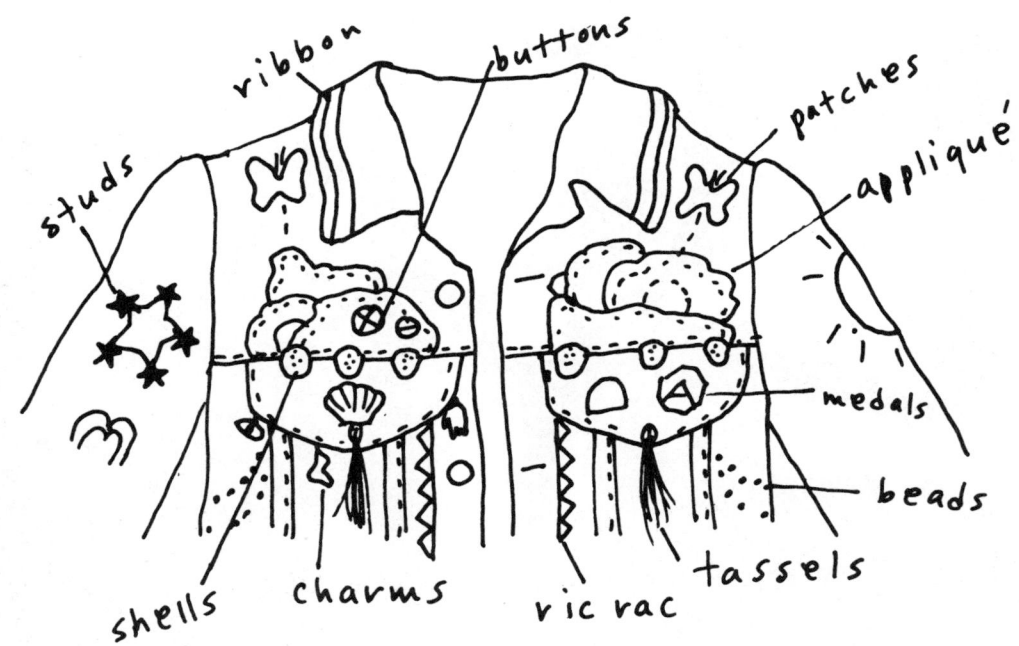

Any work of man may be a work of art, and when men are free (not necessarily economically free, but free in the sense of being responsible for the form and quality of the work they do) practically everything made is a work of art.

Eric Gill

Belt

You need: A 3" wide strip of fabric (denim, or a material of similar weight) cut on the bias, as long as your waist + 4"; a 2" strip of felt the same length; cloth scraps for appliqué; cord for ties; studs, sequins, beads, etc., optional.

Proceed:

1 Measure your waist and cut a 3" wide strip of sturdy fabric as illustrated.

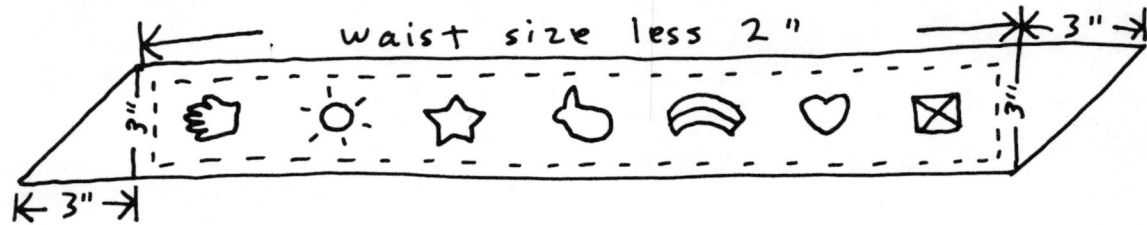

2 Appliqué with small cutouts or patches within the space indicated by dotted lines, leaving 1/2" on the top and bottom to turn under.

3 When you have sewn the appliqué in place, turn under 1/2" hem on the top and bottom and press down. Pin the 2" wide strip of felt lining on the back of the belt, covering the edges of the hem. Sew in place by hand.

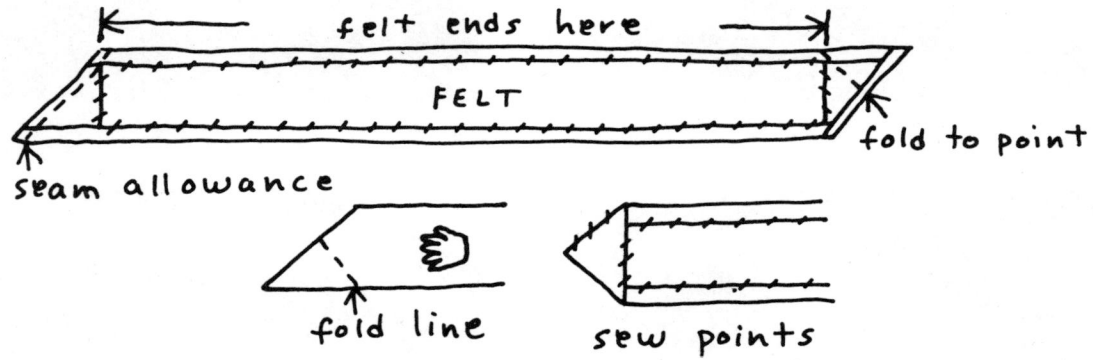

4 Turn under the seam allowance on both ends and fold to points. Trim excess fabric to make the points neat, and sew in place by hand.

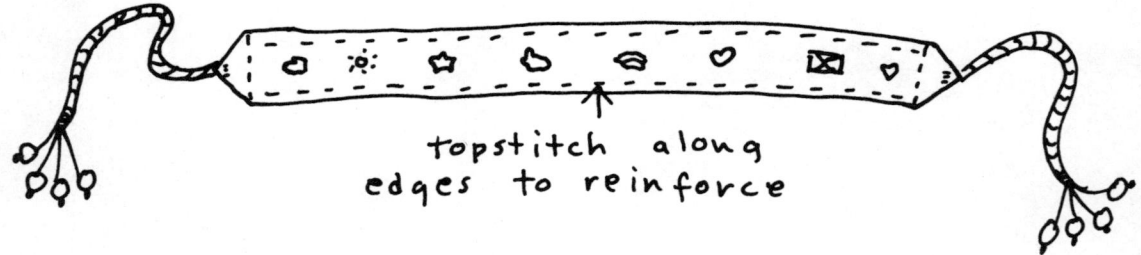

5 Secure a tie to each end with a few stitches. Jan braided three strips of thin satin cord and added beads to the ends of each one, holding them in place with knots.

You can topstitch along the edges of the belt for decoration and reinforcement.

Natural objects should be sought and investigated as they are and not to suit observers but respectfully, as if they were divine beings.

Goethe

Necklace

You need: Fabric scraps; chain or silk cord; small found objects (picture frames, charms, bells, rings, etc.); small amount of cotton or other stuffing.

Variations:

1 A very small picture frame strung on a cord or chain makes a beautiful mounting for a miniature appliqué image.

2 Cut out an image (e.g. a flower, a bird) from a piece of printed fabric. Cut another piece of cloth, any color, the same size for lining. Sew the two pieces, right sides together, leaving part of a seam open to turn. Turn right side out and stuff. Close the seam by hand. Attach to cord with a few stitches. This makes a nice setting for a favorite object or charm. Brenda put a tiny music box on hers; you might want to use a ring or a locket.

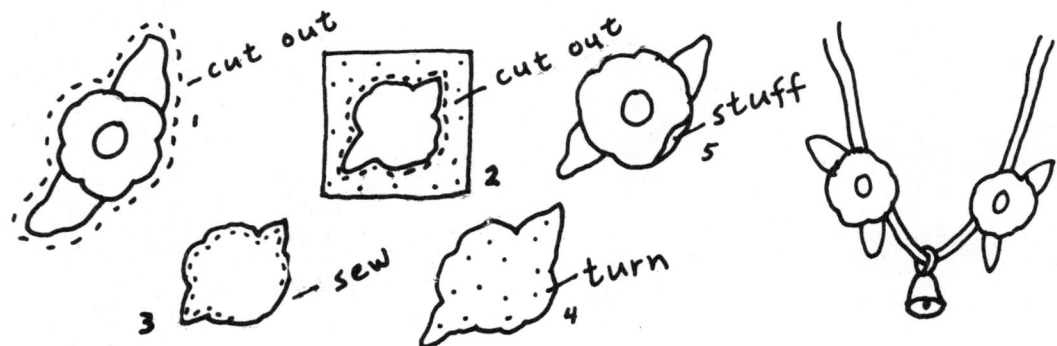

3 Cut out your own cloth shapes, line them (as above), and stuff them. Attach to cord. Keep shapes simple so they can easily be lined and turned. Sometimes stuffing small details can be difficult. Use a pencil or a knitting needle to poke the stuffing in and make points sharp. (See last page of section of color photographs.)

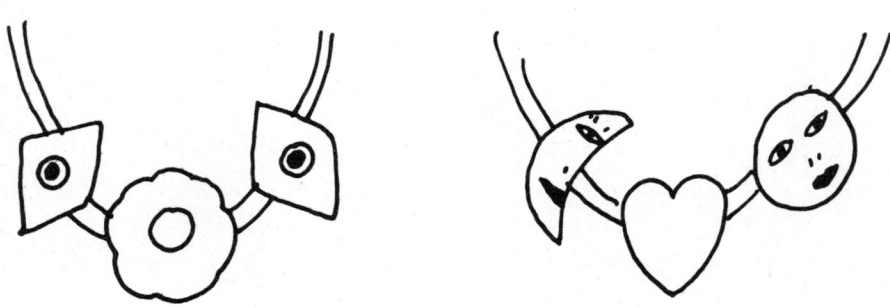

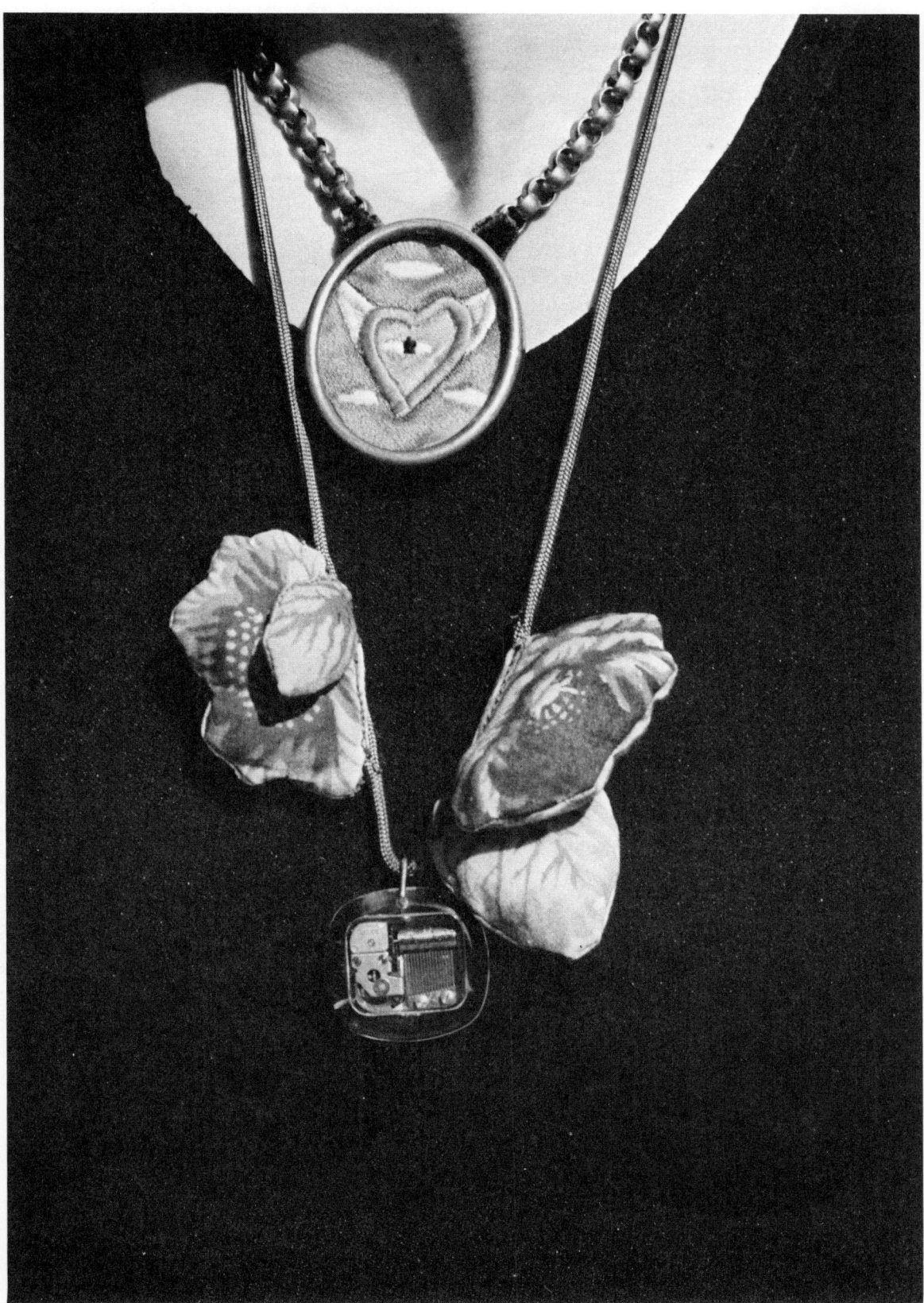

Artistic growth is, more than anything else, a refining of a sense of truthfulness.

Willa Cather

Tie

You need: 1 yard of fabric (cottons, denim, satin are all good), or you can appliqué a ready-made tie if you wish; scraps for decoration; small amount of backing material.

Proceed:

1 Make a pattern from an old tie that you have on hand (wide ties are easiest to work with) by opening the seams and pressing the two pieces flat.

2 Trace around the pattern pieces onto the fabric you are working with, center front line set along the bias of the cloth, and cut out.

3 Pin the two starred ends of the tie pieces, right sides together as illustrated, and sew.

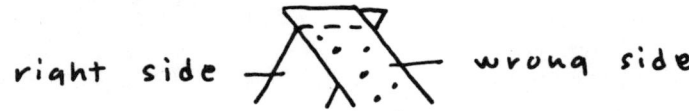

4 Press under seam allowance on the two ends and fold back to make points. Pin in place.

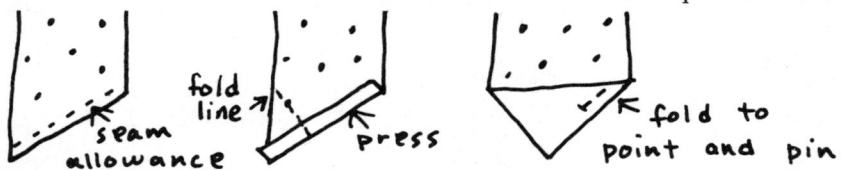

5 Lay out your design within the dotted area as shown below. Use a lightweight backing fabric under the appliqué.

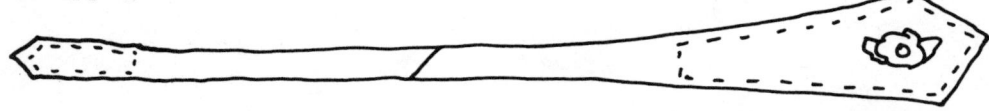

6 Remove the pins from the points and unfold points temporarily while you pin and sew the shapes in place.

7 Now, again, fold the ends back to points as you did in step 4, and this time sew the points in place.

8 Fold the tie lengthwise, wrong side out, so that the edges are right sides together; pin and sew the edges together along the seam allowance. Turn the tie right side out and press the seam flat.

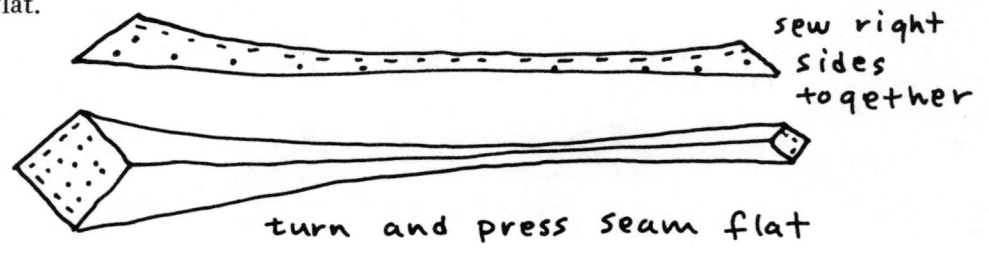

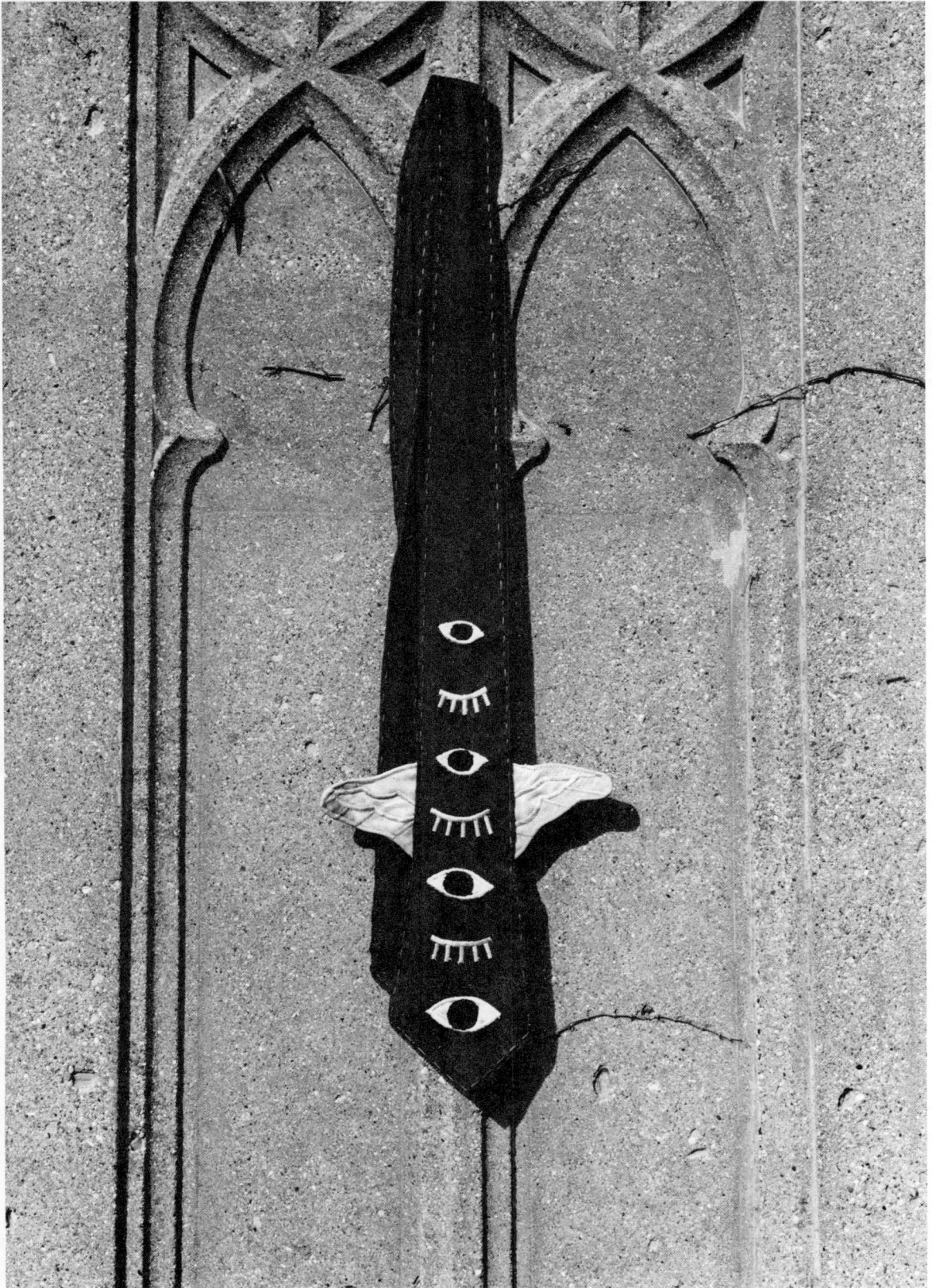

Caution is the enemy of art, and everyone is more cautious than he thinks he is.

Robert Motherwell

Vest

You need: Fabric (denim and heavy satin are good surfaces to appliqué, but any medium-weight to heavy cloth will do); buttons or other closings; pattern (you'll find simple vest patterns in the men's section of any pattern book). A ready-made vest simplifies matters.

Proceed:

1 If you are going to make the vest, you can either sew the decorations onto the fabric pieces before they are sewn together (see Dress), or you can complete the sewing of the vest and then appliqué it. If you appliqué on the finished vest, you will see the stitching on the lining side. If your stitches are neat (the tension setting on your machine must be perfectly balanced to make even stitches front and back), this can be very pretty. Try varying the bobbin thread color so that the stitching shows in multicolors.

2 Cut out your designs and place them on the vest. Make a sketch first, if you wish. Arrange them until the result satisfies you. To make a large circle patch for the back, as shown here, cut the circle to size and follow instructions given for Patches.

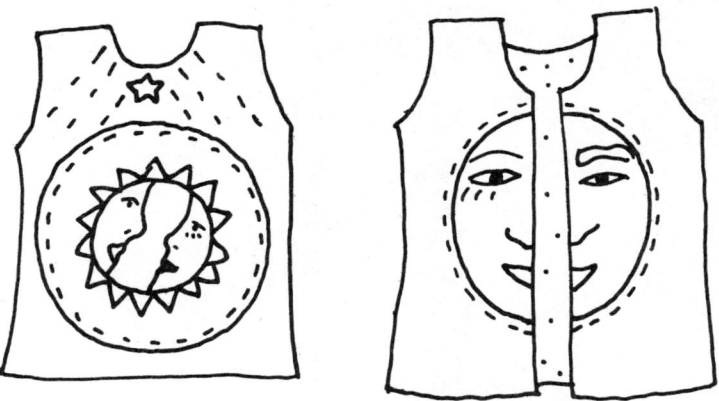

3 Pin all the appliqué pieces in place and sew with a satin stitch.

4 Finish the vest, if you are making it from scratch, according to instructions given with the pattern.

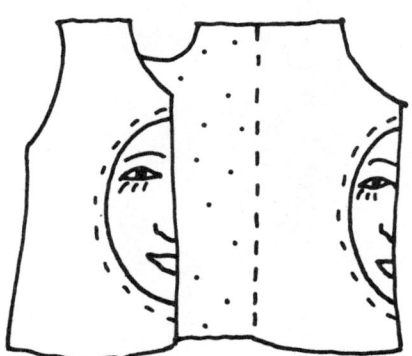

Variation: For a reversible vest, proceed according to instructions given for reversible appliqué in the Flag.

46

The appearance is not disconnected from the observer, rather it is swallowed and entwined within his individuality.

Goethe

Dress

You need: Fabric; dress pattern. Any simple pattern will do. The beginner is advised to choose one from the "easy" or "quick" section of a pattern book.

Proceed:

1 Lay out the pattern pieces on the cloth and cut according to the instructions given with the pattern. (But see 5, below.)

2 When you have cut all the pieces, spread them out and visualize the design that you would like on the dress. You may find it helpful to make a sketch.

3 Cut out the decorative shapes you have in mind and lay them on the dress pieces.

4 When your design is completed, pin all the pieces in place using backing material under each appliqué shape.

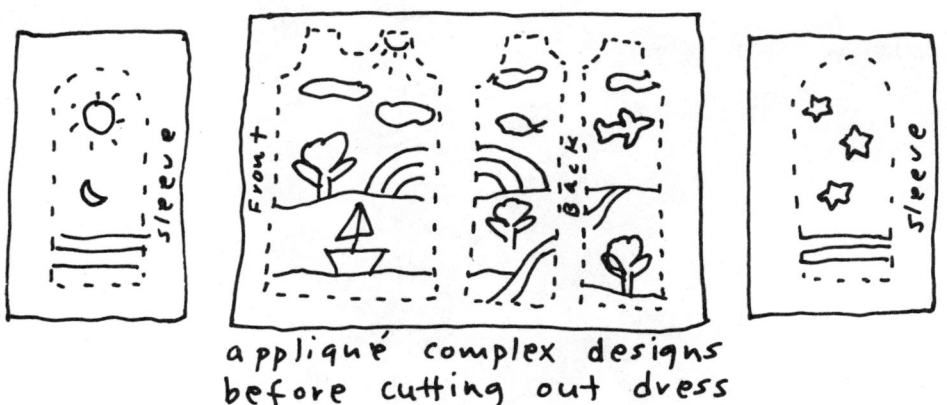

appliqué complex designs before cutting out dress

5 Sew the designs to the dress pieces with a satin stitch. (If there is to be quite a bit of appliqué on the dress, trace the outline of the pattern pieces onto the cloth first, pin and sew the appliqué within the outlines, then correct the tracings of the pattern pieces; the gathering tendency of the appliqué will misshape them slightly. Cut out the appliquéd dress pieces and proceed to sew up the dress.)

6 Sew up the dress and finish it according to the instructions with the pattern.

Variation: If you have a ready-made dress that you wish to decorate, you might appliqué the hem of the skirt, or the bodice, or the cuffs. If you want to do a more elaborate job, consider opening the seams of the sleeves or the sides, appliquéing the flat pieces, and then resewing the seams.

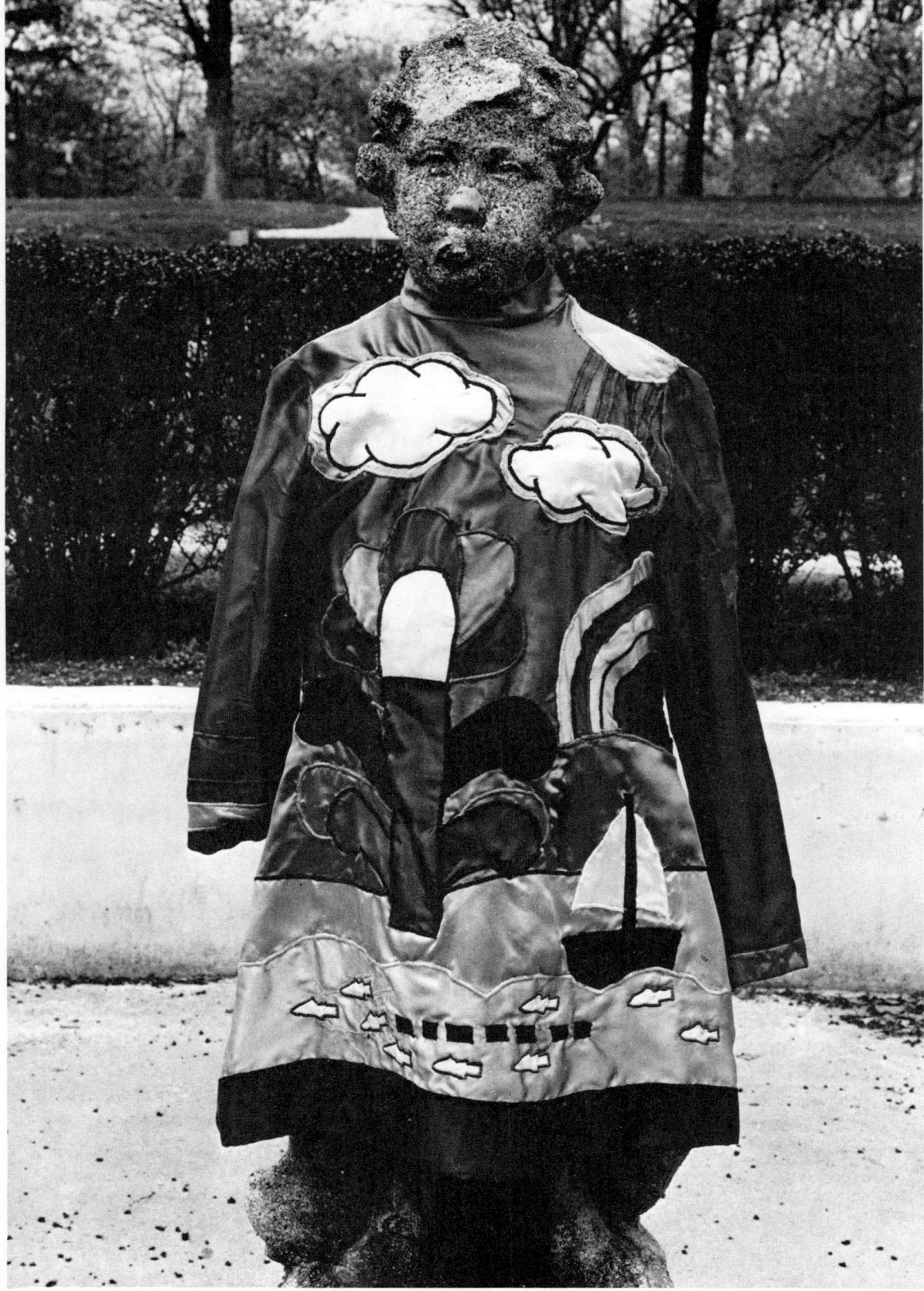

A man climbs a
mountain because
it is there.
A man makes a
work of art because
it is not there.

Carl Andre

Handbag

You need: 1 piece of fabric 22" x 27" for bag, or if you wish, two pieces sewn together to make this size, and 1 piece of fabric 22" x 27" for lining (any medium-weight fabric for bag and lining); cloth scraps for appliqué; 1 pair of 12" wooden handles (available in most notions departments and craft stores); optional quilting: 1 piece 22" x 27" polyester fill or other.

Proceed:

1 Fold bag fabric in half and mark center fold.

2 Open fabric out flat. Measure down 2" from each end of fabric and mark for roll lines.

3 Lay out your appliqué design within space indicated by dotted lines. Sew in place, using a lightweight backing fabric under the appliqué.

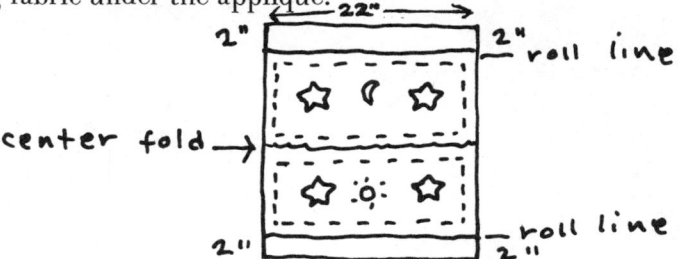

4 Optional quilting: If you want to quilt your bag, do it now. Pin the batting to wrong side of fabric and baste raw edges together. Quilt as desired by machine or hand (see pages 18 and 62).

5 Lay lining on bag fabric, right sides together. Measure down 6" on both sides of end nearest you. Mark.

6 Stitch lining to bag fabric as shown by dotted lines (below), using 5/8" seam. Clip to marks. Trim.

7 Turn right side out; press. Fold bag fabric along center fold, right sides together, toward the finished end, as shown above. Also flip over and fold the lining along center fold, right sides together, toward finished end. Right side of bag and right side of lining should be touching at raw edges. Pin. Stitch, as shown below.

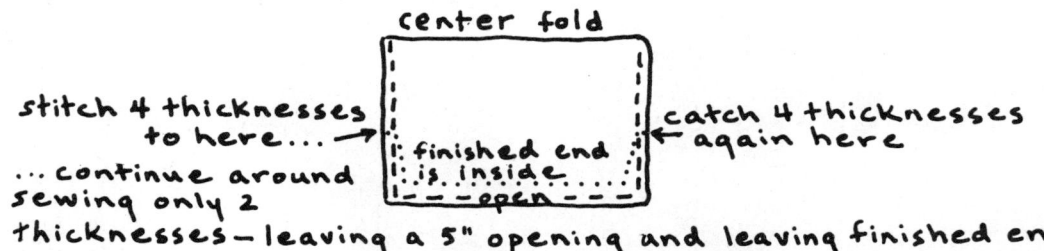

8 Turn bag through opening, turning lining to inside. Hand stitch opening edges together. Slip upper edges through handles, turning down along roll lines. Baste. Hand stitch on inside.

When you draw a tree, you must feel yourself gradually growing with it.

Chinese proverb

Tennis-Racket Cover

You need: 1 yard of medium or medium-heavy weather-resistant fabric; scraps for appliqué; 1 package bias tape; 1 1/2 yards ribbon for ties.

Proceed:

1 Lay your racket on a piece of folded fabric and draw a line along its contour, adding 3/4" seam allowance all round as illustrated.

 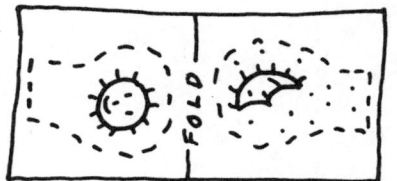

2 Lay out your appliqué design within the shape you have drawn, front and back. Pin and sew in place. (You won't need a backing if the fabric you are using is heavy enough by itself.)

3 Before cutting out the pieces of the cover, be sure the outline you have drawn has not been misshapen by the sewing of the appliqué. If it has, correct it to its original size. Cut out the two pieces.

4 Pin front to back, wrong sides together, placing the pins perpendicular to the edge so you can sew over them, and sew as illustrated.

5 To sew the bias tape around the edges, start at the bottom closed edge. Fold the tape around the raw edges and sew as you go. When you get to the opening, continue to sew the tape onto the front side of the cover. Continue sewing along the bottom, around the back, and up the back side till it meets the place where front and back are joined together. Cut the tape here and tuck the end under.

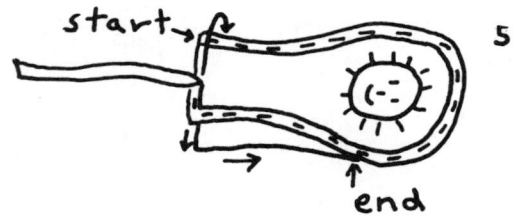 

6 Sew ribbons onto front and back to close.

Variation: An even simpler version is the following: Draw shape on folded cloth as shown below; appliqué front and back; cut out and sew right sides together. Turn and add tie.

Color helps to express light, not the physical phenomenon, but the only light that really exists, that in the artist's brain.

Henri Matisse

Mask

You need: A square of fairly stiff cloth about 1' x 1' for the basic face shape (heavy cotton or satin is good); the same amount of backing fabric (canvas, heavy cotton—something that's not scratchy); colorful scraps for details; about 1 yard of ribbon.

Proceed:

1 Cut the mask shape approximately the size of your face; cut a piece of backing material the same size and shape.

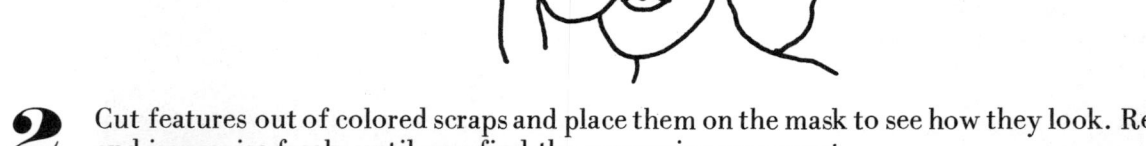

2 Cut features out of colored scraps and place them on the mask to see how they look. Rearrange and improvise freely until you find the expression you want.

3 Pin the cutouts to the mask, together with the backing material.

4 Sew the designs in place with a satin stitch. Finish the edges of the mask either by hemming or by satin stitching.

5 When the mask is sewn, mark and cut holes where the eyes will be, and finish the raw edge with satin stitching.

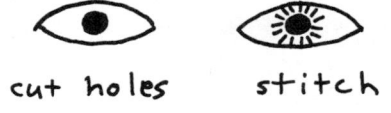

6 Attach ribbons just above the eyes, near the edge.

Metallic threads, beads, buttons, or other decorations may be applied to enhance the finished mask. In almost any good craft center or fabric store you can find a variety of fancy trims.

The world from which I draw the elements of reality is not visual but imaginative.

Juan Gris

Costume

You need: An old sheet or a length of solid-color, or print, cotton fabric (enough to cover your body); scraps for appliqué; backing fabric; ribbon; cardboard.

Proceed:

1 Put the cloth or sheet over your head so it falls evenly all around you. Make marks over your eyes and nose.

2 Lay the cloth out flat and decorate with appliqué designs, remembering that the designs for the face should be placed where you have marked the eyes and nose.

3 Pin and sew the designs in place, using a backing under each shape. If you wish to keep the area over the face flat (as we did), sew your design for the face first separately; then cut a piece of lightweight cardboard slightly smaller than the face shape. Pin the face, with the cardboard behind it, to the costume cloth at the point you have marked and sew in place.

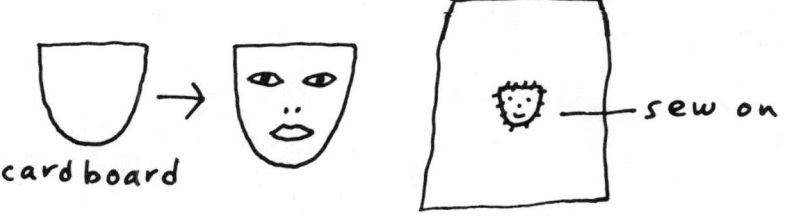

4 Cut holes through the cloth and the cardboard where the eyes will be, and satin stitch the raw edges.

Image: likeness: SEMBLANCE . . . a person strikingly like another person . . . INCARNATION . . . an illusory form: APPARITION . . . a mental picture of something not actually present: IMPRESSION . . . IDEA, CONCEPT . . . REFLECT, MIRROR . . . to make appear

Webster's New Collegiate Dictionary

Pillow

You need: Fabric (use solid colors, or prints, or combine them; choose a rather heavy material—bright heavy cotton and natural canvas are good, especially if the pillow will receive a lot of wear; if the pillow is to be primarily decorative, try velvets or satins); stuffing (shredded foam, polyester fill, or other. The amount of stuffing depends, of course, on the size of the pillow you plan to make).

Proceed:

1 Cut two pieces of fabric about 2" larger all round than you want the finished pillow to be. (Cutting the shapes slightly larger allows for seams and the stuffing that will make the pillow three-dimensional.)

2 Lay out an appliqué design on one or both pieces. Very often, a beautifully decorated front works best with a simple solid color or calico backside.

3 When you are happy with the design, pin the pieces in place and sew. Don't forget to use a backing under the parts to be appliquéd. After the sewing is done, you can elaborate the design by trapunto stuffing, or by adding free-floating ribbons (see color photograph).

4 Sew the front of the pillow to the back, right sides together, leaving one side partly open to turn.

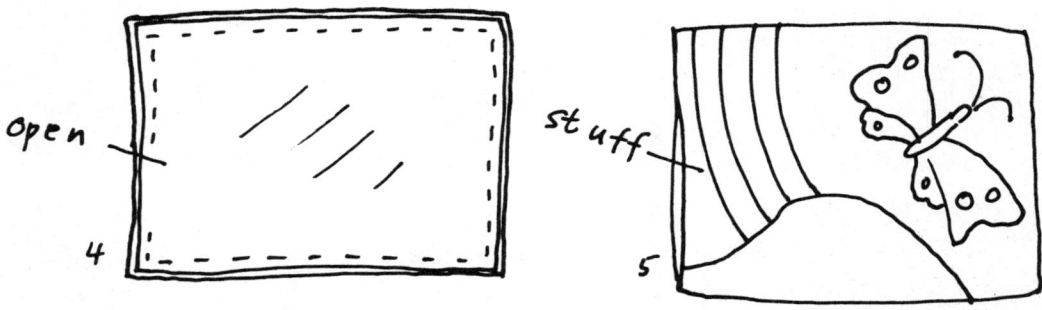

5 Turn the pillow right side out and stuff. To close the open seam, turn the edges in and sew with a simple hemstitch by hand.

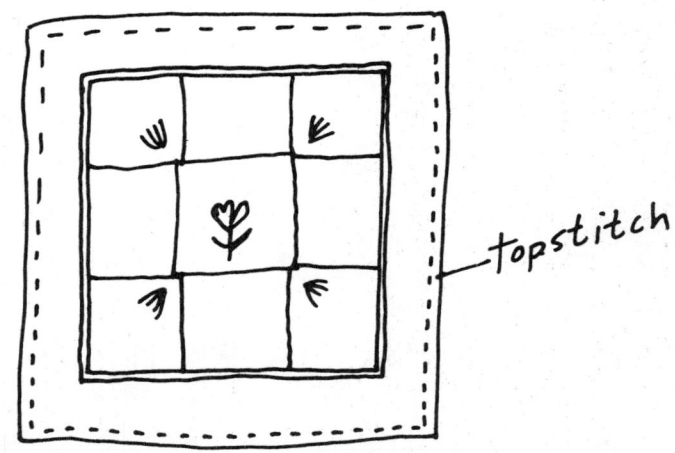

6 Topstitching about 1/4" from the edge makes a nice finishing touch. Do this before stuffing, leaving part of the seam open; complete topstitching after stuffing.

You do not need to leave your room. Remain sitting at your table and listen. Do not even listen, simply wait. Do not even wait, be quite still and solitary. The world will freely offer itself to you to be unmasked, it has no choice, it will roll in ecstasy at your feet.

Franz Kafka

Quilt

You need: Fabric (any medium-weight materials are good to use on the top appliqué side; lining fabric—to be cut or pieced to the size of the top [use a light- to medium-weight material if you plan to use a fill in between; corduroy makes a good lining if you want a warm quilt without using a fill]; backing material [canvas, heavy cotton] for the parts you plan to appliqué. The amount of fabric you'll need depends, of course, on the size of the quilt you plan to make); filling (polyester fill is washable and very good, but an old blanket will do); knotting string, optional (you can buy this in most notions departments, or use double strands of embroidery thread); wide seam binding or ribbon (at least 1 1/2" wide), enough to go around the borders of your quilt.

Proceed:

1 Measure the top surface of your bed. Also measure the distance from the top of the bed edge to the floor that you wish your quilt to cover. These figures together determine the size of your quilt. Add a few extra inches to the length to cover pillows. If you plan to do a lot of appliqué on the quilt, allow a few extra inches in both directions for "shrinking"

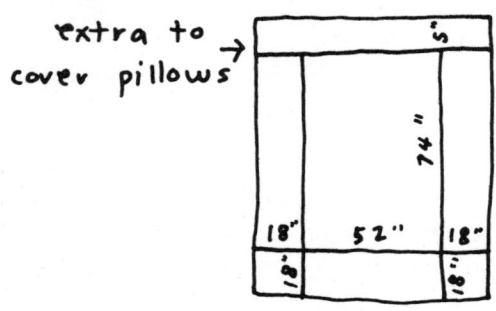
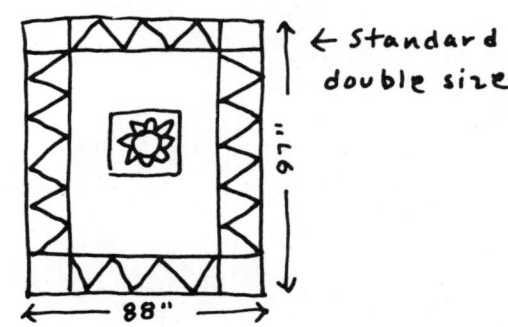

 2 Lay out your quilt in small sections that will be easy to sew. Add 1/4" seam allowance all round to each section's measurements. Cut each section from the fabric of your choice, and cut a backing the same size for each section that you plan to appliqué.

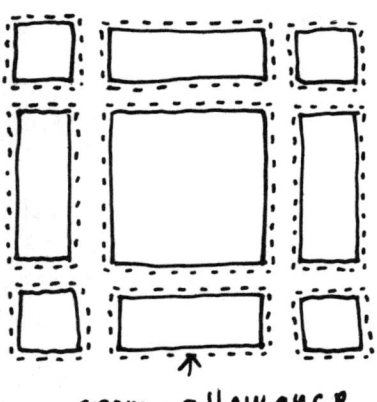

It's easiest to work on a large open floor space where you can lay all the pieces out together as you cut them.

 3 Add your appliqué designs to each section.

 4 Pin and sew the designs in place.

Art is simply a result of expression during right feeling. It's a result of a grip on the fundamentals of nature, the spirit of life, the constructive force, the secret of growth, a real understanding of the relative importance of things, order, balance. Any material will do. After all, the object is not to make art, but to be in the wonderful state which makes art inevitable.

Robert Henri

5 Pin the finished sections together and sew along the 1/4" seam allowance in whatever way is easiest for the shapes you are working with. For example, if you are working with squares, first sew the squares together in rows, then sew the rows together.

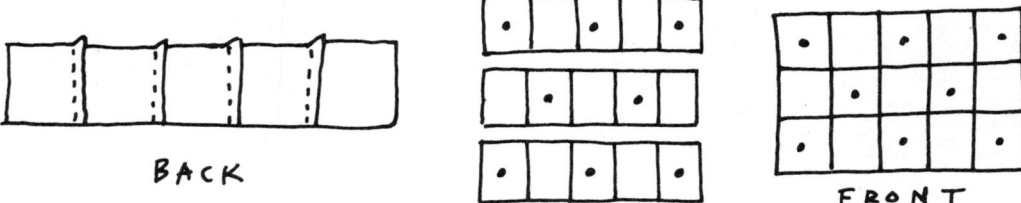

Lining the quilt:

6 Cut (or piece together) a length of fabric the same size as the quilt. Cut a piece of polyester fill, or other padding, the same size. Pin the quilt to the lining (wrong sides together), with the fill in between. Place the pins close together and perpendicular to the edges, so that you can sew over them.

7 Sew the three layers together 1/2" from the edge.

8 Secure the front to the lining by hand-quilting or by knotting, which means simply to take a stitch, by hand, through the three layers of the quilt, bring the needle and string back up very close to the original insertion point, and tie a knot. Clip the ends of the string.

Place the knots at regular, inconspicuous points in the seams and tie the knots on the lining side, or use the knots as a decorative element, tying them on the appliquéd side.

9 Enclose the raw edges in a wide seam binding or ribbon border. Place the border right sides together with the quilt and pin and sew as illustrated. Turn border to enclose the edge, and sew to the back of the quilt by hand with a hemstitch.

Variation: To make a simple quilt, appliqué only the center portion of the spread. Complete the quilt by piecing together multicolored print squares. I used scraps from all the clothes I have made and worn over the years, so that the quilt is full of nostalgic value, even though it was made recently.

Note: There are many variations on quilt making. If you wish to pursue the subject further, two wonderfully inspiring picture books about quilts are: *America's Quilts and Coverlets* by Safford and Bishop (Weathervane Books), and *The Pieced Quilt* by Jonathan Holstein (N.Y. Graphic Society).

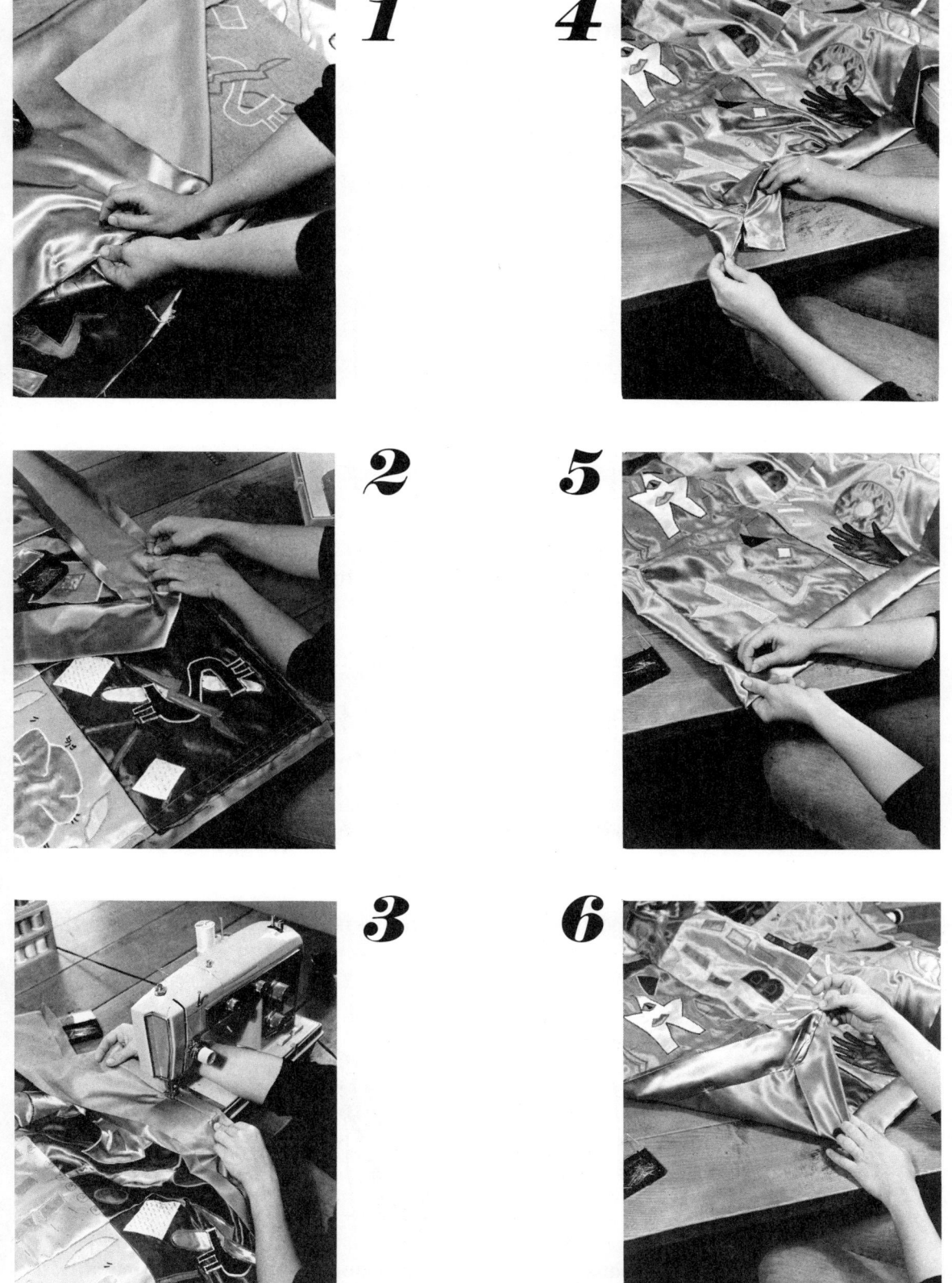

Sewing the border (1-3) and mitering the corners (4-6).

Headboard

You need: 3/4" plywood; felt (enough to cover and to appliqué); carpet tacks, or a heavy-duty staple gun; glue; stuffing, optional (polyester fill, scraps, etc.).

Proceed:

1 Measure the width of your bed. The height should be determined by how the headboard is to be attached to the bed. If your bed is free-standing, measure up from the floor; if the bed will be against the wall, measure up from where the board will attach to the bed frame or the wall. Cut the plywood to size. (Although it's a matter of taste, 2' or 3' is a comfortable amount of headboard to have extending above the top of your mattress.)

2 Cut a piece of felt the size of your board, adding at least 3" on all sides for "shrinking" and for stretching around the board.

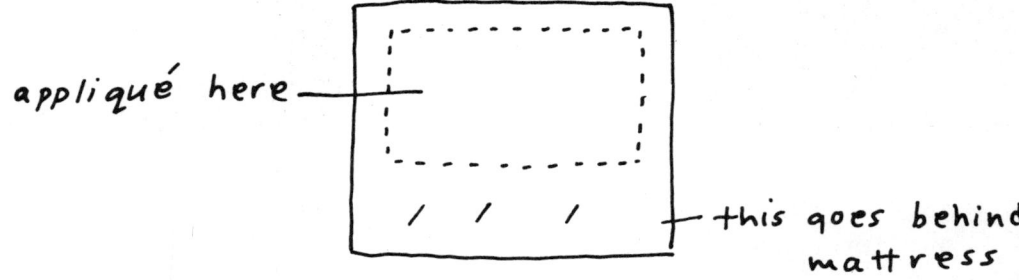

3 Lay out your design, pin the pieces, and sew in place. If you like, stuff parts of your appliqué after it is sewn: cut a slit in the fabric behind the shape to be filled, stuff, and sew the slit closed by hand. This is called trapunto.

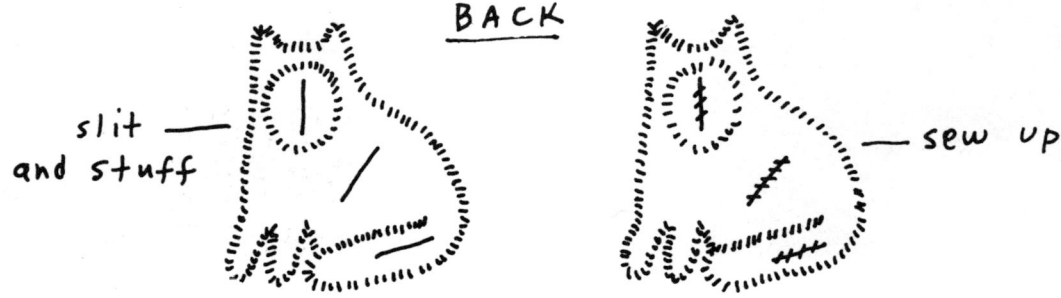

4 Stretch the finished piece around the board and attach with staples or carpet tacks. Make a contrasting edge by cutting a strip of felt 3/4" wide, long enough to go around the board. Glue it over the edge. If your bed is free-standing, you may want to cover the back with felt as well.

5 Secure the board to the bed frame with screws or nails; or if your bed has a metal frame, you can mount the headboard on the wall behind it.

How to paint the Landscape. First you make your bow to the Landscape —Then you wait and if and when the Landscape bows to you, then and not until then can you paint the Landscape.

John Marin

Standing Screen

You need: 3 or more mahogany flush doors (a standard item in lumberyards), 12" wide by 72" high; an equal number of Masonite panels 11 3/4" wide by 71 3/4" long; enough fabric to cover the doors (felt is a good material to work with as it doesn't ravel and so allows you to work the edges neatly) and small scraps of felt or other fabric to design with; two hinges for each fold in the screen; staples or carpet tacks; screws.

Proceed:

1 Cut fabric pieces the size of your doors plus 3" or 4" all round to allow for "shrinking" and turning around the edges.

2 Lay out your appliqué design on the panels of cloth, taking care to keep the design within the central area as shown here.

3 Pin and sew all the pieces in place. When the appliqué is finished you can add trapunto stuffing. For details, see Headboard.

4 Stretch the finished pieces around the doors and tack or staple to the back as illustrated. Keep the edges neat and flat; cut away any excess fabric at the corners to keep them smooth. Trim all excess material from the panels.

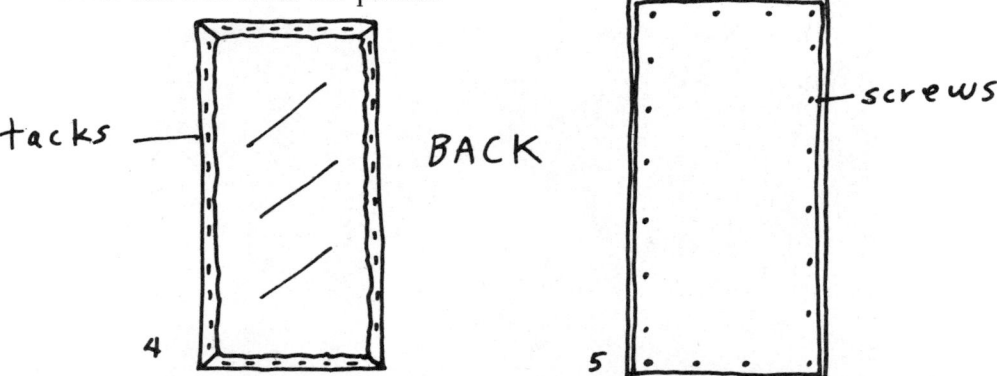

5 Place the Masonite panels (paint them first if you wish) over the back, covering the staples, and screw in place along the edges of the hollow doors.

6 Add the hinges about 6" from the top and bottom.

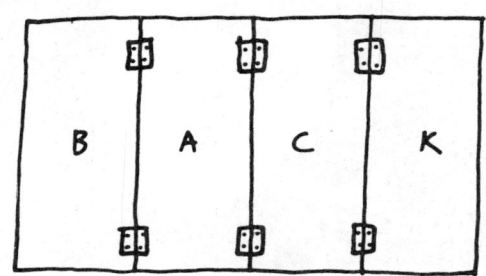

In earlier times, artists liked to show what was actually visible, either the things they liked to look at or the things they would like to have seen. Nowadays, we are concerned with reality rather than with the merely visible . . .

Paul Klee

Doll

You need: Fabric (we used pink satin, but you can use practically any color and fabric—even a calico print would be nice. Remember, cottons are washable, satins and felts are not); stuffing (old stockings, shredded foam, scraps); yarn for the hair; embroidery needle and thread; 3/4 yard of ribbon. You might want to use buttons or beads for eyes.

Proceed:

1 On a piece of folded fabric that you have selected for the body, draw the outline of a torso and head. Make it fatter than you want the finished doll to be (when the doll is stuffed it becomes round and thin), and add 1/4" for seam allowance all around. Cut out.

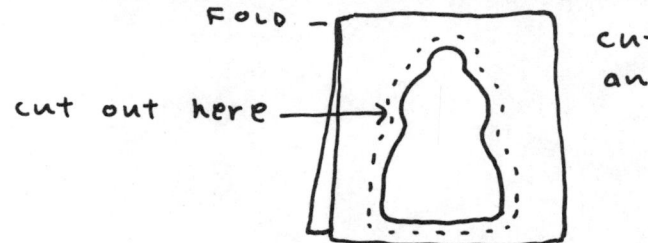

2 Now, draw the outline of the arms and legs on folded material, making them also very fat. Cut the arms at an angle across the top so they will fall to the sides of the body. Cut legs straight across the top.

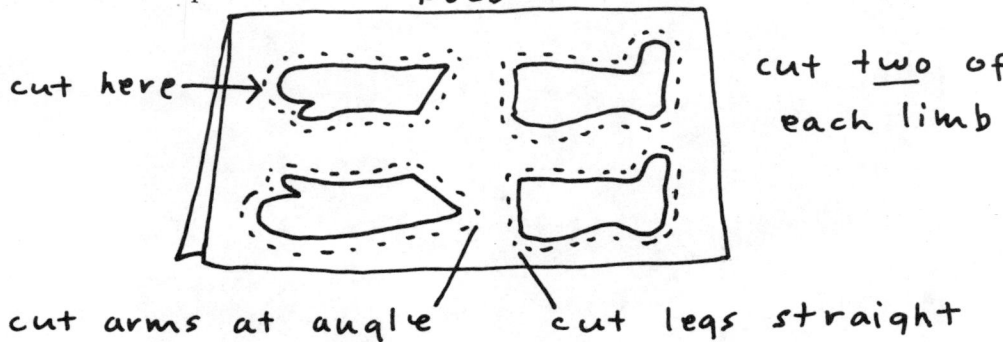

3 Place the torso front and back right sides together, and sew. Leave the bottom end open.

4 Turn the torso right side out.

5 Stuff the head and body until they are full and round, and sew the bottom edges together by hand with a small neat stitch.

6 Do the same with the arms and legs; place right sides together and sew, leaving the top open. Turn right side out, stuff, and sew the open seams together.

The eagerness of objects to be what we are afraid to do cannot help but move us.

Frank O'Hara

7 Attach the limbs to the torso with embroidery thread, making small neat stitches.

8 When the body is finished, sketch the features onto the face and body, and embroider them in by hand. Use whatever colors you like. A simple running stitch is good for outlines; use a satin stitch to fill in.

9 Attach yarn hair by threading through the head and knotting.

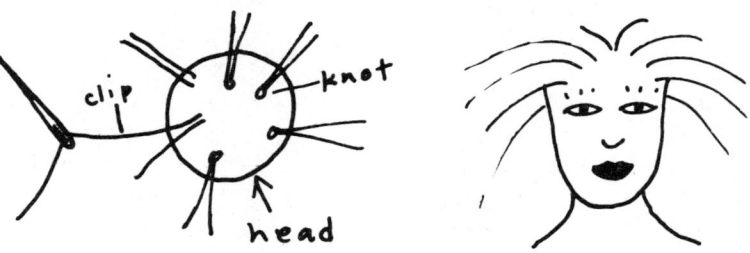

10 Dress the doll as you please. To make a cape, as shown, cut a piece of fabric this shape, making it to fit your doll as indicated. Cut another piece the same size, but in another fabric, for the lining.

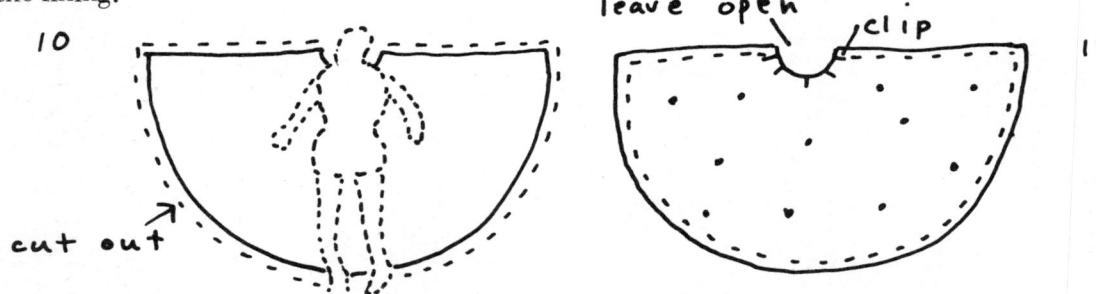

11 Appliqué designs on one or both pieces, or perhaps embroider a poem or a message.

12 Pin the pieces, right sides together, and sew, leaving the neck open.

Turn right side out. To finish the neck, clip the curve and turn in to hem. Edge with lace or a ruffle. Sew ribbons to either side of the neck opening for ties.

Suggestions: Cut out the face of a photograph, mount it on cardboard, and paste it to the head.

Embroider a child's name across the chest for a gift.

Embroider the body with tattoo designs.

There on that scaffolding reclines
Michelangelo.
With no more sound
than the mice make
His hand moves to
and fro.
Like a long-legged
fly upon the stream
His mind moves
upon silence.

W. B. Yeats

Flag

You need: Weather-resistant fabric (a heavyweight nylon works best; the background piece must be heavy enough to take the satin stitching smoothly without a backing; the directions we are giving here are for a reversible flag with the same designs on both sides—have enough scraps to appliqué two sides); grommets and seam binding, optional. If you live in a city, you can buy fabrics and bindings from a flag manufacturer.

Proceed:

1 Decide how big you want your flag to be. Cut a piece of weather-resistant fabric that size plus a 1/2" hem allowance all round.

2 Trace or sketch your designs for one side onto colored cloth. Keep the shapes very simple.

   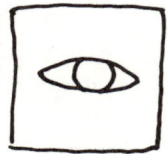

3 Cut out the shapes.

4 Pin the designs onto the background piece; at the same time, pin a square of cloth for the reverse image, slightly larger than each shape and in another color if you wish, to the background on the opposite side of each of the designs. You will have a sandwich of designs, background in the middle.

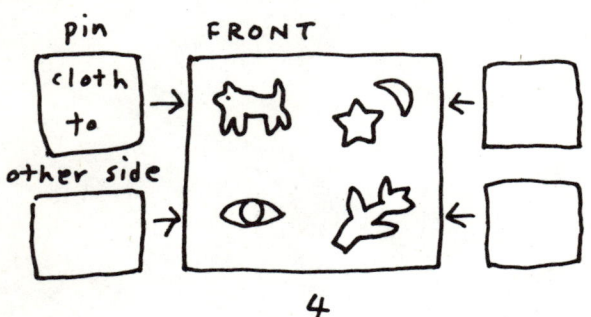 

5 Sew the designs with a satin stitch. Take care to adjust the tension properly so that the stitching is even on both sides. When the sewing is finished, cut the fabric that is not part of the design away from the background on the back, taking care not to cut into the satin stitching. Trim the edges as neatly as possible.

6 Hem the edges of the flag, or make a border with wide seam binding.

A good way to hang the flag is to apply grommets (you can buy kits in most notions departments) to the corners and attach rope. Or, tack it to a pole.

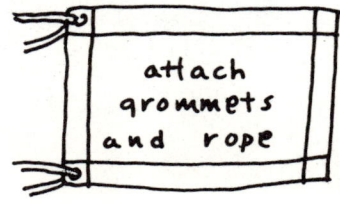 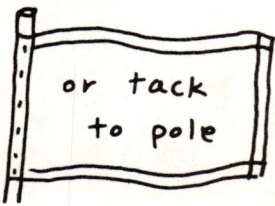

Art is a human activity consisting in this, that one man consciously by means of certain external signs, hands on to others feelings he has lived through, and that others are infected by these feelings and also experience them.

Tolstoy

Child's Project

Any child old enough to wield a pair of scissors can do this project as there is no sewing involved. The assistance of an adult is helpful, however, in the finishing stages.

You need: Colored felt; scissors; glue; found things (sparkles, artificial flowers, ribbons, buttons, etc.).

Proceed:

1 Cut a large piece of fabric—about 2′ x 2′ is a good size—for the background and spread it before you.

2 Now, imagine a scene that you would like to create. A good way to do this is to sit quietly and think of images that you particularly like. Cut them out of felt as you think of them, and arrange them on the background.

3 When you have made a picture that pleases you, glue down the pieces. You may want to add other decorations such as ribbons, colored buttons, beads, etc.

4 You may finish the piece for hanging by stretching it around a frame, by adding a seam binding, or simply by turning under and hemming the edges.

For other children's projects see Valentine and the How to See It exercises, all of which can be done in felt and glue as well.

Is the name of the sun here? —Yes. —Where? —In schools and in the classrooms. —Whereabouts in the classrooms? —Everywhere. —Is it in this room? —Yes. —Where else? —In the corners. —Where else? —In all the little corners (pointing to the surrounding air). —Where? —In the empty space. —What is the empty space? —Its made up of little paths.

Piaget questions child

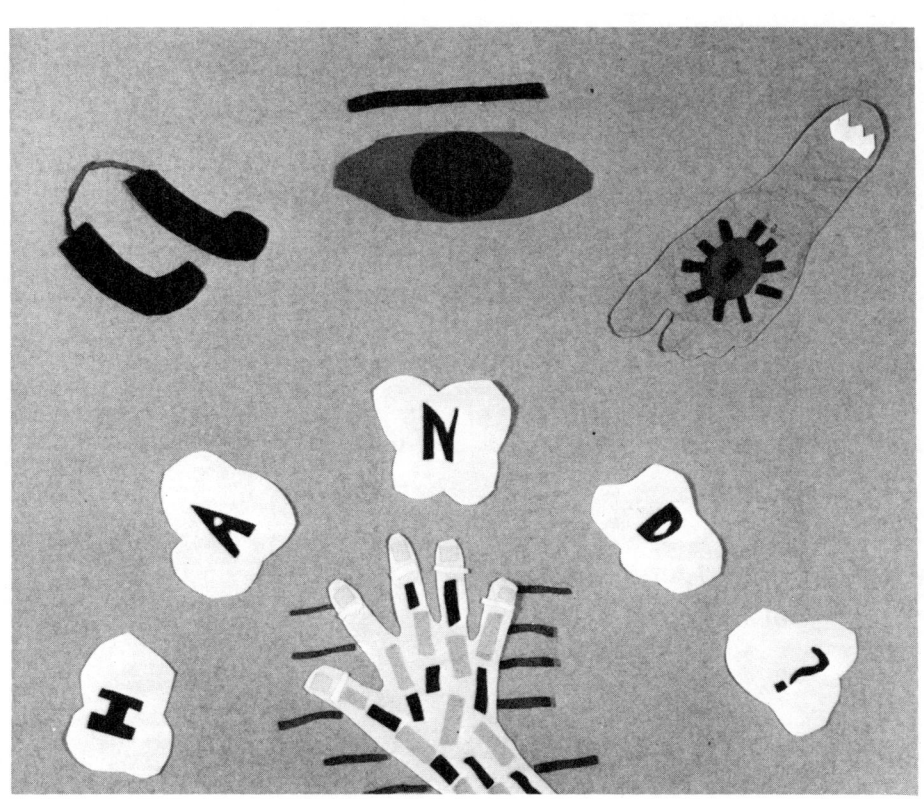

Valentine

You need: Fabric; decorative items—laces, sparkles, beads, etc., optional.

Proceed:

1 Cut a piece of fabric, with backing if necessary, for the background, whatever size you wish the valentine to be. The one we show here is big, but you may wish to make yours card size so that it would fit, folded perhaps, into a large envelope.

2 Consider the person that you are making the valentine for. What images come to mind when you think of that person? What images could act as symbols of your feelings for that person? Make sketches of your thoughts as they occur.

For example:

3 When you have decided on several images to work with, cut them out and place them on the background. Arrange them and add whatever details you feel are necessary to complete the picture.

If you wish to make letters or words part of your design, either sketch or trace letters onto cloth and cut them out, or machine or hand embroider them on the piece (see Jacket).

4 Pin and sew all the pieces in place. Finish the edges (page 18).

This is an excellent project for a child to do in felt and glue (see facing page).

The fairest thing we can experience is the mysterious. It is the fundamental emotion which stands at the cradle of true art and true science.

Albert Einstein

Poem Piece

You need: Fabric, scissors, thread, pins.

Proceed:

1 Choose a poem, or a line from a poem, that is especially meaningful to you.

2 Cut a piece of background material, with backing if it's necessary, the size that you want the finished piece to be.

3 Sit quietly, clear your mind, and contemplate the words of the poem. Don't try to think of ways to illustrate the poem; simply rest your mind on the words of the poem as a whole and wait for images to arise on their own.

When images occur to you either sketch them or cut them directly from the cloth.

4 Arrange and rearrange these elements until you have a design that reflects your response to the words.

5 To cut out letters, you can either trace them onto the cloth or draw them freehand, and then cut out. To embroider words directly on the cloth, see Jacket for details.

(w. B. yeats)

6 Pin all the elements in place and sew.

7 Hem the edges, or see Wall Hanging for other finishing suggestions.

"I'm sure (my memory) only works one way," Alice remarked. "I can't remember things before they happen."
"It's a poor sort of memory that only works backwards," the Queen remarked.

Lewis Carroll

Games

You need: Fabric; scissors; thread; pins.

Proceed: There are many variations on this project. Start by making something simple, perhaps a checkerboard. Cut a piece of fabric the size you want your game to be, and proceed in the same way as described for the Wall Hanging.

Familiar games you can make:
  Tosses   Backgammon
  Targets   Hopscotch
  Checkers   Mazes
  Parcheesi   Pin-A-Tail

Or you can make up your own. For example:

Make a visual game for a child, like Karen's Witch who becomes a Princess when you unzip her (see page 7); or a wall hanging with many pockets filled with pretty things; or a color chart or an alphabet and number chart to hang in a small child's room.

The image cannot be dispossessed of a primordial freshness, which idea can never claim. An idea is derivative and tamed. The image is in the natural or wild state, and it has to be discovered there...

John Crowe Ransom

Photo Collage

You need: Fabric; scissors; thread; pins; photograph(s).

Proceed:

1 Cut a piece of fabric, with backing, for the background, the size that you want the finished piece to be.

2 Place your photo (or photos) on the cloth and study it carefully. What other images, lines, colors, does it suggest to you? Does the picture evoke a particular story or emotion that you wish to elaborate?

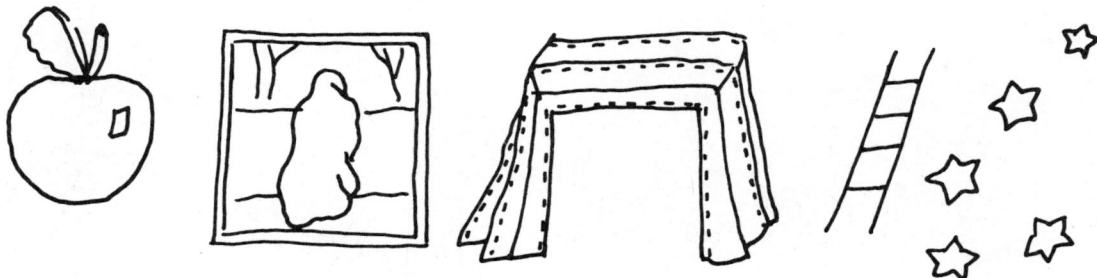

3 Cut out your designs and arrange them around the photo on the background.

4 When the arrangement pleases you; remove the photo and pin all the pieces in place. Sew with a satin stitch.

5 Now, replace the photo and glue it lightly to the fabric. Sew in place with a basting stitch (small close stitches will tear the photo).

6 Finish the edges.

A photograph is a secret about a secret. The more it tells you the less you know.

Diane Arbus

Family Portrait

You need: Fabric; scissors; thread; pins; family photographs, optional.

Variations: Trace each family member's profile onto cloth, cut out, and use the silhouettes in the design of a wall hanging as pictured on facing page, top. This is a family "Magic Carpet." The family profiles are in a descending line on the right side.

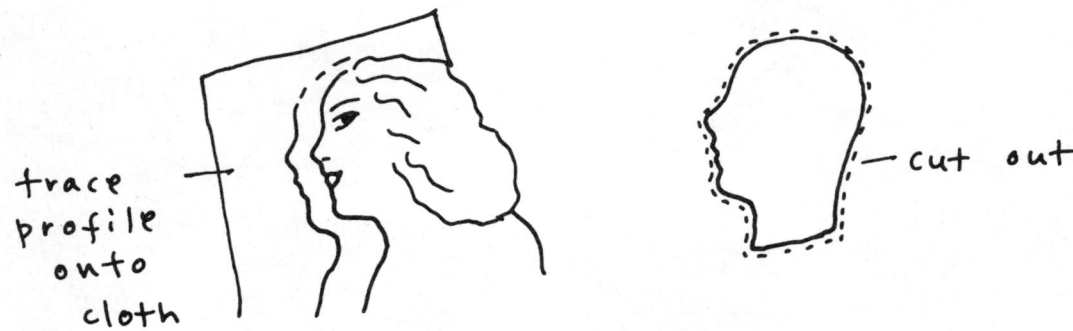

Photo collage: Cut a piece of fabric—with backing—for the background, the size you want the finished piece to be. Lay out your design, using the photographs as the central element. You may want to surround each photo with symbols or designs that you feel express the person portrayed. When the design is completely laid out, remove the photos. Pin and sew the appliqué in place. Now, replace the photos and secure them with a few drops of glue. Sew around the outside edges of the photos with a basting stitch (zigzag). If you want to cut out a shape from a photograph, cut about 1/4" outside the outline of the figure, so that it can be sewn without obscuring the edges of the figure.

Finish the edges (see Wall Hanging).

For an illustration of a photo collage see page 83.

Photo screen on cloth: If you know how to do silk screening, you can make a piece something like Sue's portrait of her parents shown on facing page. A photographic silk screen was made (your local printer will probably be able to do this for you, or can advise you where it can be done) from old family photographs; the images were then screened onto fabric. Appliqué and embroidery are the finishing touches.

What do we dream with? The eyes.

Child's response

Personal Memento

You need: Fabric; something personal that you want to place in a fabric "setting." I collected locks of my friends' hair; you might have a locket, a letter, an article of clothing, etc., that you treasure.

Proceed:

1 Cut a piece of background, with backing if necessary, the size you want the finished piece to be.

2 A nice way to dream up the design for your memento is to contemplate the sentiment the object you have chosen evokes. As images that reflect your feelings come to mind, sketch them out, or better still, cut them directly from the cloth. Lay out the images, or the abstract shapes if that is the case, around your memento and rearrange them until you have a picture that pleases you.

3 Pin all the pieces in place and sew.

4 Finish the edges by turning under and hemming, or see Wall Hanging for other ideas.

You may want to protect your memento by enclosing it in a plastic pocket. Flex-o-pane, a plastic "cloth" that is sold in hardware and plastic stores, is good for this.

You can combine ideas from this project with those mentioned for the Necklace or the Valentine.

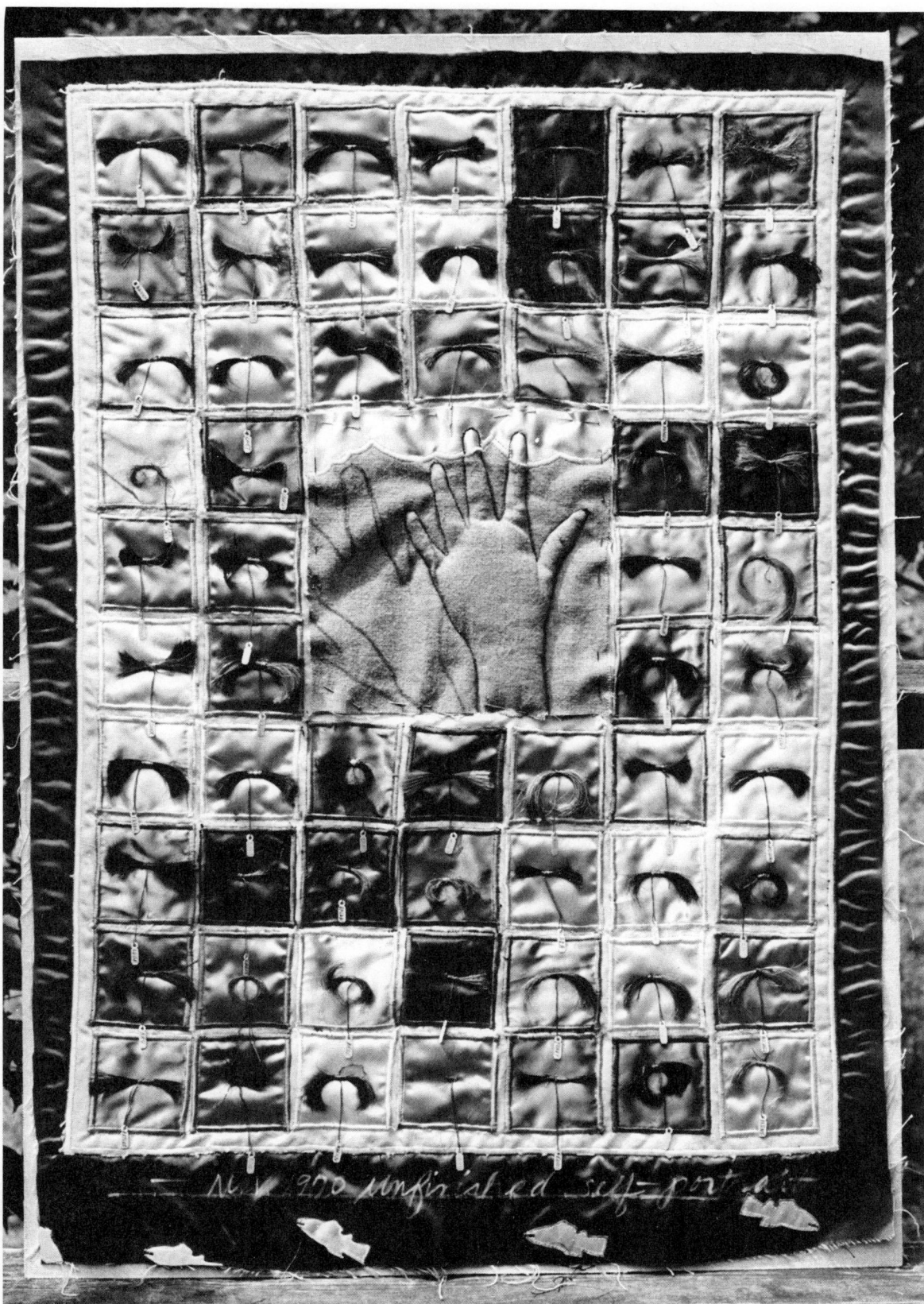

No one can draw a line that is not a boundary line; every line splits a singularity into a plurality.

Escher

Diary/Book Cover

You need: Fabric and backing.

Proceed: For this project you will make one piece for each month of the year, and then, at the end of the year, sew them all together into a fabric diary which may be used as a hanging or a quilt.

Pick images each month that illustrate your particular feelings at that time, or whatever special events have occurred during that month, etc.

It's easiest to make all the pieces the same size. Leave about 1/4" seam allowance all round on each piece, so that they can be sewn together at the end of the year. See Quilt for detailed instructions.

Variations: A single month's piece is a beautiful birthday card to give someone dear. You may want to make a piece relating to their astrological sign or to some special memory that month holds for them.

Make a cover for your present diary or any treasured book. It's nice to cover a sketchbook and carry it with you to jot down fleeting ideas or images that you may want to recall and focus on later.

1. Cut fabric to size, adding extra as shown. Turn and hem short ends.
2. Appliqué.
3. Fold over ends to make flaps, leaving enough room so that when book is closed cover fits well; draw lines indicated (book size + 1/8"); sew flaps right sides together.
4. Turn the jacket right side out, turn under seam allowance on top and bottom, and sew down. Slip book cover inside flaps.

The moment the artist identifies his work with the construction of his own life, time then ceases to be merely the place where the work is done, but becomes the work itself.

Albert Camus

Wall Hanging

You need: Fabric; backing; pole, grommets, or boards for hanging.

There are two ways to approach this; one is to have an idea before you begin of how you want the piece to look. Make a sketch if you find that helpful. The other is to make up the images as you go along. To do this, clear your mind; study the colors and prints of the fabrics you have chosen to work with. Cut out shapes and designs as they occur to you and let these images suggest others. Continue in this way until your picture develops.

Proceed:

1 Cut a piece of background material, with backing if needed, the size of the picture you have in mind and spread it out before you.

2 Cut out your designs and arrange and rearrange them until you have a picture that pleases you.

3 Pin all the elements in place and sew. If you are making a large piece (3' x 3' or more; choose a size that is easily maneuverable on your machine), lay out your design in sections that can be pinned and sewn separately, then sew these completed pieces together or attach them to the background. For example:

4 To line the finished piece, lay it flat on the floor and cut a piece of fabric (or piece together several lengths of fabric) slightly larger than your picture. Pin the picture and the lining, right sides together, along the edges. Place the pins perpendicular to the edge and close together.

5 Sew the two pieces together, leaving space open on one side to turn the piece right side out. Turn, and sew the open seam closed by hand.

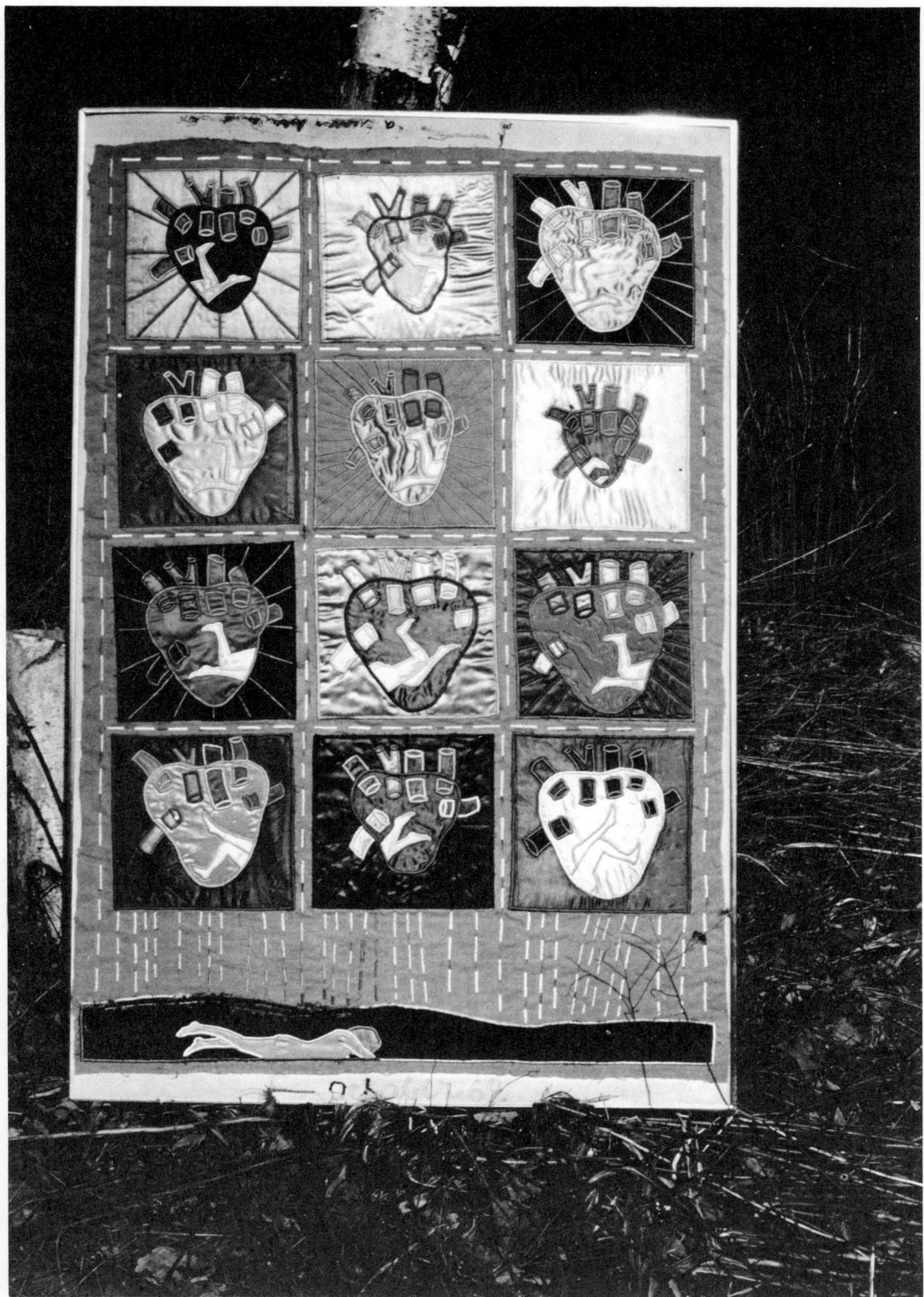

When we are actually creating a work of art, there is a sense of total confidence; our message is simply appreciating the nature of things as they are and expressing appreciation without any struggle of thoughts and fears.

Chogyam Trungpa

Topstitch 1/4" from the edge for a nice finish.

 Another method is to pin and sew the lining to the front, wrong sides together, then bind the edges with a wide seam binding or folded ribbon. This is illustrated in Quilt.

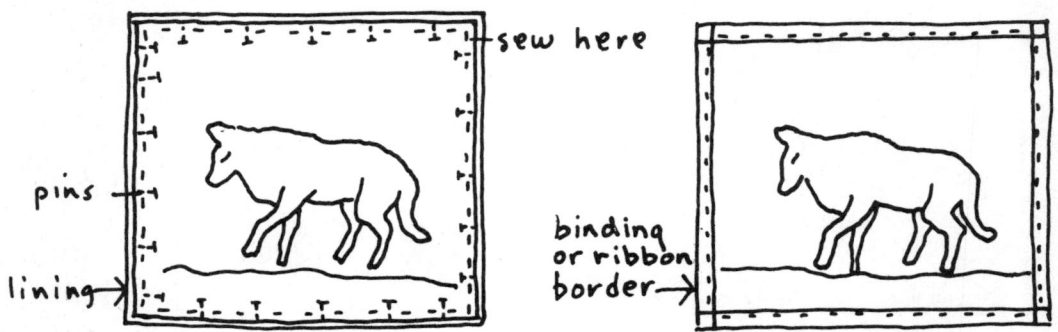

 To hang the piece: When sewing the front to the lining, leave a 2" or 3" space open at the top on either side, and insert a pole. (Get a wooden pole in any lumberyard, thick enough to hold the weight of your piece and several inches longer than the piece is wide; or perhaps use a metal curtain rod if that is more readily available.)

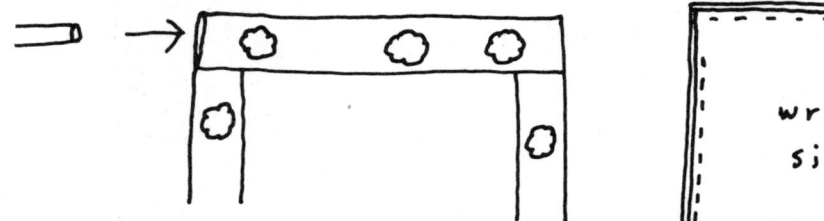

Or, sew folded strips of cloth or heavy ribbon to the back, near the top of the piece, and slip pole through.

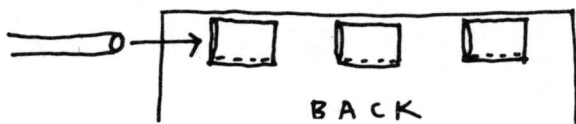

Or, apply grommets to the corners, and hang on nails.

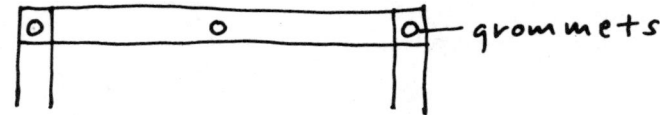

Or, place the top edge of the piece in a sandwich between two narrow lengths of board; screw or nail the boards tightly together, and then nail or hook the boards to the wall.

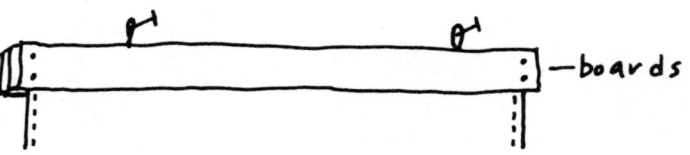

The artist: disciple, abundant, multiple, restless.
The true artist: capable, practicing, skillful; maintains dialogue with his heart, meets things with his mind.

Aztec

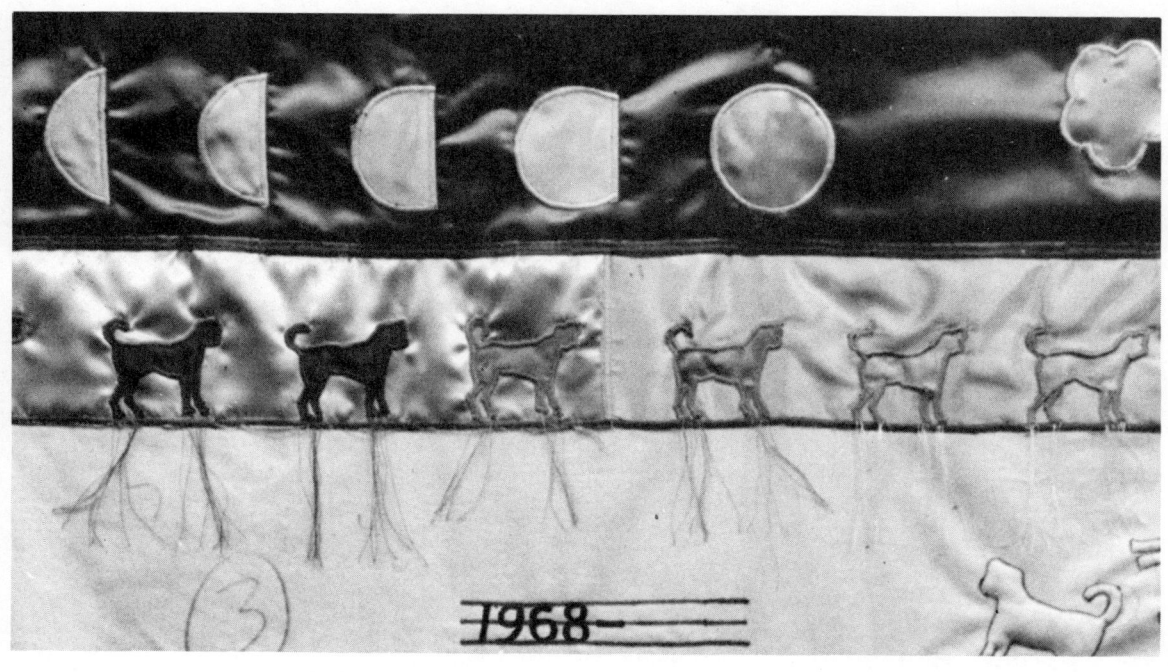

All projects by Anne Raymo except for the following: p. 7 Karen Pellaton; p. 23 Jared Reinmuth and Anne Raymo; p. 25 top Jimmy Raymo, bottom Tess Raymo; p. 29 Sue Raymo, Tess Raymo, and Anne Raymo; p. 31 Sue Raymo; p. 39 all jackets by Bill Greer and Anne Raymo; p. 41 Janet Mayer; p. 43 longer necklace Brenda Mayhew; p. 51 Peggy Pejeau; p. 57 Amy Reinmuth; p. 59 top Enid Hofsted, bottom Ann Treadway; p. 61 bottom quilt Virginia Raymo and Anne Raymo; p. 65 quilt Enid Hofsted; p. 69 doll in middle of top photo and in bottom left photo Amy Reinmuth; p. 73 Amy Reinmuth, Cristin Reinmuth, and Jared Reinmuth; p. 75 top Jimmy Raymo, bottom Tess Raymo; p. 77 Amy Reinmuth; p. 81 Norman Laliberté; p. 83 Jim Raymo and Anne Raymo; p. 85 bottom Sue Raymo. **Color section:** p. 1 Karen Pellaton; p. 2 quilt in top photo Enid Hofsted, bottom of two quilts Virginia Raymo and Anne Raymo; p. 3 ribbon pillow Mary Klicka, trapunto pillow and patchwork pillow Enid Hofsted; p. 4 jackets by Holly Vose, and Anne Raymo and Bill Greer; p. 5 wall hanging Natalie Vermann, felt and glue project and family portrait Sue Raymo; p. 8 flag Amy Reinmuth, Jared Reinmuth, and Cristin Reinmuth. **Back cover:** baby quilt Karen Pellaton; handbag Peggy Pejeau; jacket Janet Mayer; costumes Amy Reinmuth, Cristin Reinmuth, and Jared Reinmuth.

All photographs by Jim Raymo except for the following: p. 81 courtesy Norman Laliberté; p. 93 courtesy Terry Dintenfass; baby quilt on back cover and first page of color section courtesy Karen Pellaton; wall hanging on p. 8 of color section courtesy Marvin Sylvor.

Special thanks to Norman Laliberté and Terry Dintenfass.